MW00437197

PRAYERS *for the* BATTLEFIELD

STAYING MOMSTRONG IN THE FIGHT FOR YOUR FAMILY AND FAITH

Heidi St. John

TYNDALE
MOMENTUM®

The nonfiction imprint of
Tyndale House Publishers, Inc.

Visit Tyndale online at www.tyndale.com.

Visit Tyndale Momentum online at www.tyndalemomentum.com.

Visit the author online at heidistjohn.com.

TYNDALE, *Tyndale Momentum*, and Tyndale's quill logo are registered trademarks of Tyndale House Publishers, Inc. The Tyndale Momentum logo is a trademark of Tyndale House Publishers, Inc. Tyndale Momentum is the nonfiction imprint of Tyndale House Publishers, Inc., Carol Stream, Illinois.

Prayers for the Battlefield: Staying MomStrong in the Fight for Your Family and Faith

Copyright © 2018 by Heidi St. John. All rights reserved.

Cover illustration of arrows copyright © Anastasiia Gevko/Shutterstock. All rights reserved.

Designed by Julie Chen

Edited by Stephanie Rische

Published in association with William K. Jensen Literary Agency, 119 Bampton Court, Eugene, Oregon 97404

Unless otherwise indicated, all Scripture quotations are taken from the *Holy Bible*, New Living Translation, copyright © 1996, 2004, 2015 by Tyndale House Foundation. Used by permission of Tyndale House Publishers, Inc., Carol Stream, Illinois 60188. All rights reserved.

Scripture quotations marked NIV are taken from the Holy Bible, *New International Version*,® *NIV*.® Copyright © 1973, 1978, 1984, 2011 by Biblica, Inc.® Used by permission. All rights reserved worldwide.

Scripture quotations marked NASB are taken from the New American Standard Bible,® copyright © 1960, 1962, 1963, 1968, 1971, 1972, 1973, 1975, 1977, 1995 by The Lockman Foundation. Used by permission.

Scripture quotations marked ESV are taken from *The Holy Bible*, English Standard Version® (ESV®), copyright © 2001 by Crossway, a publishing ministry of Good News Publishers. Used by permission. All rights reserved.

Scripture quotations marked NKJV are taken from the New King James Version,® copyright © 1982 by Thomas Nelson, Inc. Used by permission. All rights reserved.

Scripture quotations marked CEB are taken from the Common English Bible, copyright 2011. Used by permission. All rights reserved.

Scripture quotations marked ICB are taken from the International Children's Bible.® Copyright © 1986, 1988, 1999 by Thomas Nelson, Inc. Used by permission. All rights reserved.

Scripture quotations marked GNT are taken from the Good News Translation in Today's English Version, Second Edition, copyright © 1992 by American Bible Society. Used by permission.

Scripture quotations marked ASV are taken from *The Holy Bible*, American Standard Version.

For information about special discounts for bulk purchases, please contact Tyndale House Publishers at csresponse@tyndale.com, or call 1-800-323-9400.

ISBN 978-1-4964-1277-5

Printed in China

24	23	22	21	20	19	18
7	6	5	4	3	2	1

To the memory of my grandmother Eunice,

whose fierce love for God's Word

and dedication to passing that love on to her

grandchildren is still bearing fruit today.

And to every mother who prays that someday

the same will be said of her.

Take courage! The battle is the Lord's.

Contents

Section 3 — WISDOM *for the* BATTLEFIELD

Section 4 — WEAPONS *for the* BATTLEFIELD

Section 5 — FOR *the* WEARY WARRIOR

Section 6 — BEYOND *the* BATTLEFIELD

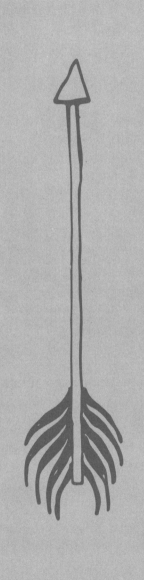

Be strong in the Lord and in his mighty power. Put on all of God's armor so that you will be able to stand firm against all strategies of the devil. For we are not fighting against flesh-and-blood enemies, but against evil rulers and authorities of the unseen world, against mighty powers in this dark world, and against evil spirits in the heavenly places. Therefore, put on every piece of God's armor so you will be able to resist the enemy in the time of evil. Then after the battle you will still be standing firm.

EPHESIANS 6:10-13

I was well into motherhood when I began to realize that Ephesians 6 is more than a poetic prelude to a far-off struggle: it's a window into the unseen battle for the very soul of humankind. The spiritual battle that's being fought today has been stripped down to one core skirmish: the fight for truth. Can you feel it? When it comes to the hearts of this generation, truth is in the crosshairs.

As a young girl, I remember my grandmother taking every possible opportunity to speak God's Word to my heart. I wasn't always listening, but she spoke it anyway. Sometimes she would speak soft truths to me as I drifted off to sleep. And when she prayed, her prayers were filled with affirmations from Scripture. I remember how she prayed for wisdom, admitting that she had no wisdom apart from God. When she corrected me, her words were strong and commanding—as if she were preparing me for the battle of my life.

Because she was.

I've been raising our seven children for nearly twenty-eight years, and now I'm a grandmother too. When I look into the eyes of my grandsons, I think of the countless times when my grandmother focused her declining energy on my siblings and me. She knew what every mother and grandmother needs to know right now: our children are worth fighting for. They're worth the tears you cry over them, worth the sleepless nights, worth the prayers you send heavenward on their behalf, and worth the investment you make into teaching them the ways of the One who made them.

After all, it's His ways that lead to victory.

Your children have been entrusted to your care at a pivotal point in history. We are at a cultural crossroads, and the battle for the hearts and minds of our children is raging all around us—even in our churches.

The stakes are high; in fact, they're eternal. Make no mistake: the enemy of your soul is playing for keeps.

I wrote most of the pages of this book with tears in my eyes because I'm acutely aware of my own need to stay on the battlefield for the sake of my children and grandchildren. I know that victory won't be handed to us easily, but with the Lord's help, the battle can be won.

Beloved, there will be times when you speak truth to your children and they won't listen. They may drift off to sleep while you pray over them, or they may roll their eyes at your attempts to train them in the ways of the Lord. But don't give up! My grandmother knew that no matter whether I seemed interested or not, God was at work.

God is still at work. He loves you. You belong to Him. Like Esther, you were born for such a time as this—and so were your children.

As you read *Prayers for the Battlefield*, you will see that it is divided into six sections. Each section is filled with devotions and prayers designed to meet you wherever the battle takes you. The index at the end of the book is intended to help you look up a prayer based on the struggle you're facing. Whether you find yourself in need of courage, hope, rest, or perseverance, my prayer is that you'll find life within these pages.

As you read this book, I'm praying that you will shout

a battle cry on behalf of your children. They carry with them the promise of a new generation of warriors—warriors trained to recognize the voice of truth.

Onto the battlefield! The battle belongs to the Lord!

—*Heidi St. John*
FALL 2018

ONTO *the* BATTLEFIELD

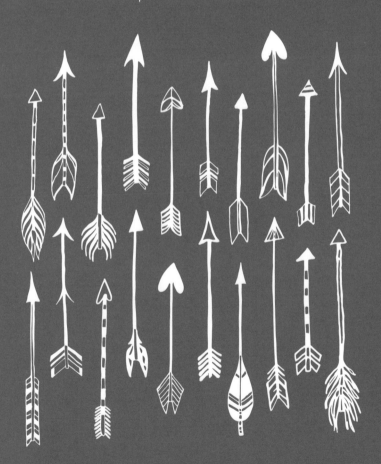

IN *the* TRENCHES

A PRAYER *for the* RELUCTANT WARRIOR

We are not fighting against flesh-and-blood enemies,
but against evil rulers and authorities of the unseen
world, against mighty powers in this dark world,
and against evil spirits in the heavenly places.

EPHESIANS 6:12

*H*ave you noticed that we tend to live in a state of reactive Christianity? When we're not experiencing some crisis in our lives, it's easy to forget about the war that Paul is warning us about in Ephesians 6. When we're feeling safe and comfortable, we can quickly forget that the war is still raging around us.

There was a time in my life when I paid little attention to the spiritual side of mothering, choosing instead to focus my energy on meeting the physical demands of our family. I lived a comfortable Christianity, like most of my friends from church. Not too hot, not too cold—just right for the culture. My motto was

"Live and let live." I didn't understand all this talk of a "war" that I kept hearing about in Sunday school. Surely that was overdone, right? Surely it wasn't *that* big of a deal.

For years I read my obligatory daily devotions, checking off this task on my to-do list like "laundry" and "vacuuming." I made sure the children went to church and stayed away from anything obviously wrong, like voodoo or Ouija boards, and I felt basically secure in my culturally correct Christianity. I didn't take the Bible's repeated warnings about the need to be spiritually prepared too seriously. I didn't want to *see* the battle, much less engage in it.

Today most of us Christians don't get onto the battlefield until the war gets out of control and someone calls for reinforcements. We are startled to attention when there's a school shooting or a national tragedy. When that happens, we hurry up and get our prayer on, showing up to candlelight vigils and praying fervently around our dinner tables. But when the crisis dies down, we hang up our helmets and go back to the status quo.

It's easy to put off confronting the enemy until we feel we have no choice, but our kids need us to engage consistently, with the holy intention of doing battle in the heavenly realms.

Don't wait for a crisis to get onto the battlefield,

precious mom! A pattern of "crisis equals prayer" puts us on the defensive and leaves us unprepared for battle. It's time. Time to get off the bench and onto the battle-field. Let's go on the spiritual offense for the sake of our children. If God is for us, who can be against us?

THE STRUGGLE IS REAL, LORD—but I suppose You already know that.

I never imagined it could be this intense . . . I must not have been really listening when I learned it would be. Somehow I never imagined I'd find myself in a spiritual battle—at least not one with stakes as high as these. I never imagined that my own children would be in the battle. If I'm being honest, I don't want to fight. I don't want to be part of this battle at all.

Sometimes I can fool myself into thinking there isn't a fight raging around me. Would You open the eyes of my heart so I can discern truth from fiction in this crazy, upside-down world? Would You help me teach my children that because the enemy of their souls is real, the war is real too? Would You help me be an example to those who look to me for guidance and protection? Help me to show them that You are the true source of guidance and protection.

I'm lazy sometimes, God . . . but I know You already know that. Please help me not to come to You only when the fighting is fierce. I want to be prepared for battle, but I confess that sometimes I struggle to put on my helmet and engage with the world around me.

Lord, I need Your wisdom and courage to stay in the fight. It's tempting to sit on the sidelines—it feels safer. *Don't let me live to be safe!* Instead, help me live to bring glory and honor to You.

Show me what I need to do to engage in the battle and not grow weary. Give me Your wisdom as my children struggle to discern who the real enemy is—and help all of us to stay true to You and Your Word. Lord, would You protect my heart from thinking my role in the battle isn't that important? Would You protect me from being complacent in my faith? Would You remind me that You are by my side?

I don't want to grow weary in doing good; I long for renewed vision to fight for what's at stake. Give me Your heart so that I will stay in the battle until the day You call me home.

Thank You for the privilege of being Your child and for fighting on my behalf. Thank You for opening my eyes to the very real battle for the heart and soul of a generation that needs You . . . starting with my own children. For their sake, I am answering Your call to engage in the battle. I'm reporting for duty, Sir!

Onto the battlefield!

Praying the Scriptures:

Psalm 1; Romans 8:31; Galatians 6:9

A PRAYER *for the* MOM
WHO FEELS BURDENED

If God is for us, who can ever be against us?

ROMANS 8:31

*I*f we are going to be victorious in the battle between good and evil, we need to know our adversary. Satan's name reveals much about his character. The title Satan is used fifty-two times in the Bible. It literally means "the adversary" or "the one who opposes." He is also called the devil, a word that is used more than thirty times in the Bible and means "slanderer" or "accuser." Regardless of what name he is called, the point is clear: we have a real enemy who wants to take us down.

Satan is a lot of things, but he isn't stupid. The Bible teaches that he operates according to a plan or a scheme (see 2 Corinthians 2:10-11 and Ephesians 6:11). He sets traps for God's people, and he will try to test us (see Luke 22:31-32). He knows our weaknesses and sends specific temptations to derail us from our Kingdom purpose. His mission is to lie to, accuse, and oppose God's people. He's quite a formidable enemy.

Satan is as stealthy today as he was in the Garden of Eden. His efforts to twist what God calls evil into good are being embraced everywhere we turn—even in the church. Sadly, we often don't notice the lies until they are deeply embedded in the fabric of our churches and families. Peter warns that there will be many false teachers in the world—and he's right (see 2 Peter 2:1).

Over the course of twenty-five years in public ministry—as well as in our personal lives—my husband, Jay, and I have often sensed the presence of the enemy. Sometimes his attacks are obvious, and other times they come in subtle ways. The enemy may try to drag us down through a heaviness of spirit—a feeling of oppression that we can't shake. Or his attack may come through a series of trials that cause us to focus on our struggles instead of on the tender voice of God.

Why is this helpful to know? Because when we know the tactics of our enemy, we can be on the lookout for him. The next time you find yourself in a situation that causes you to behave in a way that doesn't please God, stop and ask God for wisdom. Is it possible that your adversary is actively opposing you? Are you being tempted? If so, put on the armor of God (see Ephesians

6:10-20)! Victory is ultimately assured to every believer when we walk in a manner that pleases God.

Our children need to see that we trust in the power and plan of our Creator. Rather than react to the schemes of the devil in fear and timidity, we can get on our knees and expect the Lord of heaven's armies to come to our defense.

The way we respond to the devil says a lot about our faith in God. Our children are watching us. Even grown children watch to see how their parents respond to difficult times. Will we act in fear or faith?

Every day—we get to choose.

LORD, I CONFESS that sometimes I don't see the devil. I am such a sucker.

I forget that I have an adversary. I don't always recognize my enemy. Forgive me for not being more vigilant, for not keeping watch as You asked me to.

When difficult things happen, I am not prone to prayer. I am prone to worry. I sometimes forget that You are God and You are bigger than any adversary I will ever face. Thank You that Your Word says the devil will not prevail; he will be cast into the lake of fire. The enemy will not get the last word!

Help me to show my children what it looks like to be on guard against the accuser. Help me to come to You as soon as I realize I am falling for a scheme of the devil. Father, help me be the woman, the mother, You call me to be—a woman who stands strong against evil and temptation.

Lord, protect my children from the schemes of the devil too. Protect their hearts, their eyes, and their desires. Father, Your Word tells us that there are many false teachers in the world today, and I know that the only way we will be able to recognize them is to hold them up against Scripture. Remind us to be in your Word every day. Let it be a lamp to our feet and a light to our path.

And one more thing, Lord. I realize that I am prone to wander from Your truth and Your teaching even when the devil isn't prodding me. I confess that I often sin not because I don't know better but because my flesh is weak. Help me to listen for Your still, small voice, and strengthen me by Your Spirit.

Praying the Scriptures:

2 Corinthians 2:10-11; Luke 22:31-32; Isaiah 5:20; 2 Peter 2:1; Ephesians 6:10-18; 1 Peter 5:8-11; 1 Corinthians 16:13; Revelation 20:10; Psalm 119:105; 1 Kings 19:12

RUN *to the* ROAR

A PRAYER *for the* MOM
WHO FEELS OVERWHELMED

> Moses called to Joshua and said to him in the sight
> of all Israel, "Be strong and courageous, for you shall
> go with this people into the land which the LORD
> has sworn to their fathers to give them. . . . The
> LORD is the one who goes ahead of you; He will be
> with you."

DEUTERONOMY 31:7-8, NASB

Do you ever feel overwhelmed by the rapid changes happening in the world around you? If so, you're not alone. Not only that, but the battle you're facing isn't new. The good news is that we can learn from the generations of warriors who have gone before us how to bravely face our adversary.

As the apostle Paul was waiting to connect with fellow travelers in Athens, he was so moved by what he saw happening around him that he couldn't help but bring God into the conversation:

Paul, standing before the council, addressed them as follows: "Men of Athens, I notice that you are very religious in every way, for as I was walking along I saw your many shrines. And one of your altars had this inscription on it: 'To an Unknown God.' This God, whom you worship without knowing, is the one I'm telling you about.

"He is the God who made the world and everything in it. Since he is Lord of heaven and earth, he doesn't live in man-made temples, and human hands can't serve his needs—for he has no needs. He himself gives life and breath to everything, and he satisfies every need. From one man he created all the nations throughout the whole earth. He decided beforehand when they should rise and fall, and he determined their boundaries.

"His purpose was for the nations to seek after God and perhaps feel their way toward him and find him—though he is not far from any one of us. For in him we live and move and exist. As some of your own poets have said, 'We are his offspring.'"

ACTS 17:22-28

It's easy to want to tiptoe onto the battlefield, especially when the terrain we (or our children) are entering is full of spiritual land mines. We want to tread lightly for a variety of reasons: fear, insecurity, pride. But check this out, precious mom! The terrain Paul was running onto wasn't much different from the battlefield we are on today. Paul was surrounded by people who were hostile to the gospel message. Surely he had reason to stay home and keep quiet, but instead he took advantage of every opportunity to engage with the culture.

Two things in this passage should calm our fears and enable us to run onto the battlefield with confidence. First, Paul saw an opportunity to run to the roar, and he took it. The beautiful truth that Paul boldly proclaimed to the Athenians is not an easy one. He didn't shy away from telling them the straight-up truth about the world they lived in (and the world we live in): God is in control of everything that exists, and He is not far from any of us—in fact, He has chosen to be near us.

Second, Paul reminded an unbelieving, potentially hostile crowd that we live at God's pleasure. In Him, we live and move and exist. He satisfies our every need. After all, He created everything, He's big enough to handle every problem, He can answer any question, and He can calm every fear. That's a message worth sharing!

We live in a culture that is crying out for hope and change. We look to elections, social medial personalities, pastors, and teachers for hope, but Paul says that the help we are so desperate for is not far away. God is sovereign (meaning He possesses ultimate power), and He wants to help us live faithfully in the midst of circumstances that are beyond our control and even our understanding.

IT'S SCARY OUT THERE, LORD. I want to protect my kids.

It's comforting to know that You have a plan for the nations and that You have a plan for me and for my children . . . but still. My faith muscles are weak. I often doubt my ability to be like the apostle Paul. But then I remember that it wasn't Paul—*it was Your Spirit in Paul.*

Fill me with Your powerful Spirit, Lord. Help me to look for opportunities to proclaim Your truth like Paul did. Help me to model what it looks like to run to the roar of the battle with confidence in You alone. Help me to show my children what it looks like to be bold in my defense of Your creation and Your Word.

You are sovereign, and because of Your power over sin and death, I don't have to be afraid. You said that You are with me and will provide everything I need to live according to Your Word. Thank You, Lord, that we can take refuge in You.

Help me to teach my children that You have a plan—and that it's good. Remind me of Your unending faithfulness so that I can then remind my children.

The world needs You, Jesus. It needs Your hope, Your change, Your encouragement, Your wisdom. Today, as I head out onto the battlefield, fill me with joy, not timidity. I believe that You have not given me a spirit of timidity, but of power, love, and a sound mind. I trust You for every battle that's ahead.

Praying the Scriptures:

Acts 17:22-28; Isaiah 41:1-20; Psalm 5:11;
Jeremiah 29:11; 2 Timothy 1:7

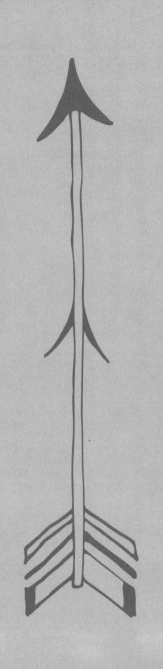

WHEREVER *you* GO

A PRAYER *for the* MOM
in NEED *of* SUPERNATURAL HELP

He will order his angels to protect you wherever you go. They will hold you up with their hands so you won't even hurt your foot on a stone.

PSALM 91:11-12

"*M*om, are angels real?" My four-year-old looked at me squarely. Blonde curls framed her inquisitive eyes. Her expression told me I needed to put down my laundry basket and sit for a bit.

There comes a time when children become very aware of the battlefield around them. All seven of the children born to Jay and me arrived with varying degrees of interest in spiritual warfare, and this particular child has always had a deep sensitivity and interest in the things of God.

I put the basket onto the counter and scooped her up into my arms. I have a rule when it comes to answering challenging questions from our children, especially when they are very young: I answer until they stop asking. I figured this would be a one-line answer and she'd be off playing with her dolls again. I was wrong.

"Well, yes," I said. "They are."

She paused. "Who made the angels? Why can't I see them? Are they good? Was Satan really an angel?" The questions went on and on before we got to the deeper issue: fear. She had seen an image that frightened her, and her imagination was kicking into overdrive. Just like her mother, she needed reassurance that God was on her side.

Kids are usually more aware of the evil in this world that we give them credit for. And there are plenty of opportunities for them to get a glimpse of evil, from magazine covers in grocery store checkout aisles to the images that scroll by on the kids section of Netflix. Pictures of real-life tragedies are constantly present on the news and online. It's part of living in a fallen world.

Our kids need to know that God loves and protects them—and part of the way He does that is through angels. Hebrews 1:14 gives us the clear purpose for angels: "Are they not all ministering spirits sent out to serve for the sake of those who are to inherit salvation?" (ESV).

When Jesus was describing the Kingdom of God to His disciples, He told them they needed to come to Him with childlike faith, and He even talked about the unique divine protection children are given:

Beware that you don't look down on any of these little ones. For I tell you that in heaven their angels are always in the presence of my heavenly Father.

Matthew 18:10

God created angels to worship and serve Him, but they have another amazing purpose: to care for and protect God's children.

What an awesome thought.

LORD, THANK YOU that You are with me wherever I go. Thank You that You promise to strengthen and help me.

Thank You for the faith of my children. Lord, I confess that I don't always have the kind of faith that looks beyond my circumstances to the very real presence of Your heavenly helpers. Would You give me more childlike faith as I shepherd my children through their struggles with fear? Would You give me answers beyond my earthly wisdom?

In Your Word, You promise that Your people can find shelter and rest and safety in You. You promise that You will rescue my children and me from every trap, every snare, and every disease. Because of You, we don't need to be afraid of anything, by day or by night. If even lions and snakes are under Your command, then surely nothing else on this earth can faze You! Thank You for that promise to rescue Your children when we call on You.

Lord, You have said that You will rescue those who love You. Would You please protect my children and me and draw us into a deeper trust in You? When we call on You, let us hear You answer. When we are in trouble, please rescue us and honor us. I'm clinging to Your words that You will give those who love You a long life and salvation.

When my children look into my eyes, I don't want them to see doubt or confusion or fear—I want them to see You. However imperfect my actions, however insecure I may be about things I am facing, would You shine through me?

Help me to take advantage of every opportunity to pour into my children. Give me insight into struggles that my little ones may not be able to give voice to so I can tell them of Your wonderful grace and mercy. Help me to see beyond the facades that my teens sometimes put up so I can walk in loving relationship with them through each season of their lives.

More than anything, Lord, I want my kids to know that You are real. Please don't let me forget to tell my children about Your faithfulness in my own life, even through times of struggle and disobedience.

Praying the Scriptures:

PSALM 91; HEBREWS 1:14; MATTHEW 18:10;
ISAIAH 41:10; EPHESIANS 5:16

> Be strong and courageous, and do the work. Don't be afraid or discouraged, for the LORD God, my God, is with you. He will not fail you or forsake you.

1 CHRONICLES 28:20

I love God's Word for many reasons, but at the top of my list is this: it shows that God can handle our humanity. He understands we are made of dust, because He is the one who breathed life into that dust in the first place. Aren't you glad? God doesn't expect us to come to Him with everything figured out. No, He desires that we lay it all out there: our worries, our fears, our doubts.

In today's spiritually polarized culture, many Christians have forgotten that the God we serve is more powerful than any force in the universe! In fact, we serve the God who created the universe, from the smallest atom to the largest star. Because we are loved and known by our Creator-God, we can have hope in the midst of any fearful situation. Psalm 27:13-14 puts it this way: "I have sure faith that I will experience the LORD's goodness in the land of the living! Hope in the LORD! Be strong! Let your heart take courage! Hope in the LORD!" (CEB).

Do you struggle to find the courage to share your faith on the battlefield? Ask the Lord to help you remember that He is destined to defeat anyone who opposes Him. Our fears, no matter how big they may seem, are no match for the Lord of heaven's armies. Listen to the words of Moses as he commissioned Joshua to take his place as leader of the Israelites. Moses knew the Israelites were about to face the battle of their lives, yet his confidence was sure: "Be strong and brave. Don't be afraid of them. Don't be frightened. The Lord your God will go with you. He will not leave you or forget you" (Deuteronomy 31:6, ICB).

God's strength shines best when we bring our weaknesses to Him and simply say, "I can't, but You can." Let God determine the outcome of the battle you're facing today. When fear meets faith, the true victor will be seen—and His name is Jesus.

STEADY MY HEART, LORD.

I want to be a light for You, but I'm afraid.

It seems that everywhere I turn, those who follow You are being challenged. I know Your heart, Lord, but when I'm given a chance to share it, my own heart races, and my hands sweat. I used to think that persecution for Your name would never happen here, but now I realize that it is a very real possibility. I'm starting to see that suffering may be part of Your plan for me—or for my children.

I love You, Lord, but when I think of the way the world is shifting under my feet, I wonder if, like Peter, my fear would drive me to deny You. I wonder if I can stand up to criticism or if I would crumble at the first sign of rejection. You were rejected, Lord, but I don't want to be! Honestly? I want to be liked. I don't want to suffer.

You said not to worry, Lord, and even though I know tomorrow will have its own set of challenges, I can't help but put myself there, in tomorrow's worry. I worry for my family. The thought that my children might face rejection because of their faith has exposed a weakness in me that I need to deal with head-on.

You said to be "strong and courageous," but then You said, "do the work." I confess that I can't do the work You have for me when I'm worried about facing rejection. Oh, how I want to please You, Lord! David said that when he cried out to You, You made him bold. I want to be like David.

Would you make me bold too?

I have so much hope because of You—please help me to share it with others freely and without fear. Give me opportunities to bless others with the message of the gospel. Let those opportunities be ordinary and extraordinary, ordained by You, for such a time as this.

Help me to be a light at the grocery store, at the mechanic's shop, at the doctor's office . . . anywhere hurting people are, Lord. Help them to see You in me. Help me to speak Your truth, filtered only by Your

Holy Spirit. Help me to speak Your truth in love. Allow me to be a part of the healing that You are doing in the lives of other people.

I need Your strength and courage. Remind me, Father, that Your Word has the power to set me free from every form of fear: fear of failure, fear of rejection, fear of making a mistake, fear of saying the wrong thing, fear of loneliness, fear of trusting others, and even fear of trusting You.

Steady my heart, Lord. Give me the courage to share my faith in a world that is hostile toward the cross. May the miracle of Your grace be ever on my lips.

Praying the Scriptures:

PSALM 27:13-14; DEUTERONOMY 31:6; MATTHEW 5:14-16;
MATTHEW 6:34; 1 CHRONICLES 28:20; PSALM 138:3; 1 PETER 3:15

A PRAYER *for the* MOM WHO WANTS *to* SET *a* GOOD EXAMPLE

Dear children, let us not love with words
or speech but with actions and in truth.

1 JOHN 3:18, NIV

I've been speaking and teaching God's Word to women
for more than two decades. But several years ago, during
a time of trial and testing in my life, the Lord opened
my eyes to an uncomfortable truth about myself: God
showed me that I wasn't a woman of discipline. Ouch.
(Insert long, painful look in the mirror.)

Upon self-reflection, I realized that I was giving
ground to the devil through my lack of spiritual discipline. I struggled (and still do, if I'm honest) to make
time for prayer and studying God's Word every day—
not because I couldn't find the time, but because I was
living in reactionary faith—only getting into the battle
when the 911 calls came. Bottom line? I was lazy, and I
was modeling lazy faith for my children.

Here's the thing: warriors can't afford to be lazy. A warrior who isn't able to wield her weapon will soon find herself unable to defend against her adversary. The problem comes when we don't see our walk with God as a spiritual discipline. The devil loves a lazy Christian because he knows that a woman who isn't in the Word struggles to have spiritual eyes. And more than that, he knows that we can't give our kids what we don't have.

We've all heard it said that ignorance is bliss, but every mom knows that ignorance is anything *but* bliss (unless you really don't want to know that your kids are coloring your bathroom wall with the *one* Sharpie you didn't see on your desk). The consequences of not noticing the Sharpie are temporary. The consequences of not studying God's Word and walking intentionally with Him carry eternal significance.

If we want to be victorious in our mothering, we need to gain the upper hand in the battle. We do that by embracing a life of spiritual discipline. We do that by allowing God into every aspect of our lives: what we watch, what we eat, what we say. It's all part of walking in right relationship with our Creator. If we're going to train our children to choose the way of righteousness, we must be willing to do the soul-changing work that shows itself in a life of self-discipline.

It's not enough to give our walk with God lip service. We need to be disciplined about our time with the Lord. Discipline is an action, not an attitude. God desires attitudes that are followed by actions.

And discipline doesn't have to be drudgery or obligatory obedience. When God meets us, the fruit of His Spirit always follows—and one of the most miraculous of these is joy.

God is worthy of our time. We can come to Him with the confident assurance that what His Word says is true: the result of walking with Him is growth, peace, wisdom, and joy.

I'VE GOT ALL KINDS OF EXCUSES, LORD.

I can list a bunch without a moment's hesitation. I'm tired. There are dishes to do; there's laundry to fold. I don't know what I'm going to do for dinner tonight, and we're out of toothpaste, so I need to go to the store. I haven't had time to myself in such a long time. Yet despite my excuses, I know that without You, I am weak and often unwise.

First Timothy 4:7 says, "Discipline yourself for the purpose of godliness" (NASB). That's what I want, Lord. I want all the blessings that are given to those who follow Your way with intention. Help me to discipline myself so I can be effective, first for You and second for my children.

Help me to be disciplined by the power of the Holy Spirit. Help me to keep my eyes on becoming more like You in every area of my life, not because these disciplines are godly in and of themselves but because they lead to godliness. At the end of the day, that's what I need. That's what my children need.

My children need me to be like You. They see me reacting in my flesh so often, Lord. I need Your help to be the wife, mother, daughter, sister, and friend that You would have me be. I recognize that this desire in me is not generated apart from Your Holy Spirit.

Help me to live my life in response to the gospel. I know that it's not enough to receive Jesus Christ as my Lord; I also need to continue to walk in Him. Give me a desire to grow more like You and seek Your Word in every area of my life.

This isn't easy for me, Lord. Sin tangles me up, and it seems my flesh is constantly at war with Your ways. But thank You that Your Spirit in me is greater than anything the devil can throw at me. And thank You that because of Your power, I can be disciplined. Because of Your power, I am an overcomer! And by Your grace, I can set an example so my children can be overcomers too.

Praying the Scriptures:

GALATIANS 5:22-23; 1 TIMOTHY 4:7; COLOSSIANS 2:6; 1 JOHN 4:4

Section 2

MY CHILD, GOD'S ARROW

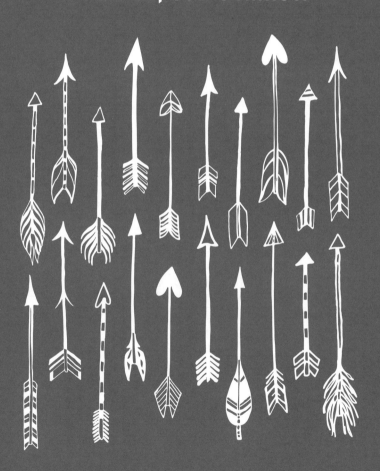

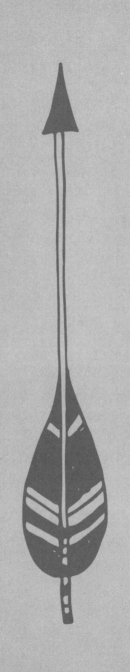

ARCHERY 101

A PRAYER *for the* MOM
WHO IS SCARED *to* LET GO

Like arrows in the hands of a warrior
are children born in one's youth.

PSALM 127:4, NIV

*T*he biblical imagery of children as arrows may sound a little strange to modern ears. After all, we spend a lot of time trying to convince our kids *not* to use objects as weapons! On the other hand, arrows are kind of hip these days. We wear them as jewelry and hang pictures of arrows on our walls. In fact, one of my favorite shirts is covered in—you guessed it—arrows. But I wonder if, even for all this imagery, we've forgotten the incredible spiritual correlation between arrows and mothers. According to God's Word, you are a warrior, and your children are like arrows in a warrior's hands. An arrow is an offensive weapon, designed to hit and penetrate a designated target. This is powerful stuff—a reminder that our children are part of an epic struggle between good and evil, a spiritual battle that has been going on for thousands of years.

Years ago, I received a precious gift from the son of my friend Ann Dunagan. She had heard me speak on the imagery of Psalm 127 several years earlier. This passage describes how God sees us as we raise His children for the Kingdom. The next time I saw Ann's son Mark, he presented me with a sculpture that really is worth a thousand words. The sculpture beautifully depicts a husband and wife dressed for battle. If you looked closely, you'd notice that my husband stands at the ready, sword and shield drawn. Several arrows from the enemy have pierced that shield, but I'm not far behind my husband. Under the watchful protection of my warrior-husband, I'm doing exactly what the psalmist David says to do: I'm launching our arrows.

This is one reason why it's so important to guard your marriage: together, you are the first line of defense for your children. The devil knows that if he can worm his wicked way into your marriage, he'll have a better shot at your kids. And really, that's what the war is over—the hearts and minds of our kids. I believe this is why the battle for marriages is raging all around us. An entire generation hangs in the balance.

Our job as parents is to put our spiritual, physical, and emotional energy into getting God's arrows (who are on loan to us) ready for battle. I'm always telling parents, "Your kids aren't boomerangs! They're not sup-posed to come back!" We only get one shot (usually!) at launching our arrows. We need to make it count.

So what does it take to prepare an arrow to fly fast and far? It takes time and intention. Arrows don't fly true unless they've been carefully and skillfully readied to do so. We sculpt our arrows for battle with the liv-ing, active Word of God, even as we steady our hearts to release them into the world.

This might sound like a daunting task, but be encour-aged: God has put the right arrow with the right warrior. Your children were intentionally placed in the hands of their warrior-mother. And God has given you exactly the tools you need for this assignment. The Bible is the lamp for your warrior feet and the light for your warrior heart. You and your children were born for such a time as this!

I DON'T FEEL VERY WARRIOR-LIKE, LORD.

In fact, sometimes, I just want to keep my arrows close. I don't want to make sure my arrow flies true; I want to keep it safe. My mother's heart is primed to protect and nurture, not to raise and release . . . and yet that's what You've asked me to do. I don't like to think about the world my children will be released into, but I trust You. I believe that I am a warrior. Help me live with this belief always in mind. Because I believe, I will step onto the battlefield with my bow raised high.

It's not every day that warriors are born, but today a trembling, newborn warrior is coming to Your throne room. I am humbled to serve the Lord of heaven's armies. I'm ready to learn how to shape my arrows to fly true. True to Your Word. True to the unique plans You have for them. True to whomever they marry, if that's part of Your plan. True to You.

Lord, I know that marriage, by your design, is a covering for our children as we raise them for You. Will you protect my marriage? Give me eyes to see any fault lines in the fabric of our family. And when I see them, give me the grace to address them with love and tender honesty. Help me not to run from trouble but to face it head-on, knowing You will never leave or forsake me.

Sometimes I wonder why You give inexperienced women like me the privilege of raising Your children, but I want to train them well. Help me to shape my arrows with good teaching. Help me to immerse them in Your Word. May they fly far and true, and may they have an eternal impact for the Kingdom.

Remind me that like Esther, we were born for this. Right kids, right mom, right time. Give me wisdom as I notice the little bends in each arrow that might prevent them from flying true. Give me patience for the times when I feel like I can't lift my bow. Give me peace for when the battle seems more than I can bear. And give me courage to release my arrows when the time is right.

Praying the Scriptures:

PSALM 127; PSALM 119:105; ESTHER 4:14

CAPTURED

A PRAYER *for the* MOM IN NEED OF RESCUE *from* SEXUAL SIN

I will give up whole nations to save your life,
because you are precious to me.

ISAIAH 43:4, GNT

*H*ave you ever been in love? I'm not talking about small love here—I'm talking about the kind that makes your palms sweat and your heart pound. I'm talking about a love that *captures*. There are few emotions in this world that are as intoxicating, especially with love's power to draw one person to another. I still remember seeing my husband as I walked down the aisle on our wedding day. My heart was (and still is) captured by him.

Being captured can be the best thing ever.

But it can also be one of the worst things, depending on who or what we've been captured by. The Bible teaches us that our decisions come down to what attracts our eyes and captures our hearts. This was true of Eve, who was captured by the thought that she could be like

God (see Genesis 3:5). She and Adam chose to disobey God, opting instead to listen to the lies of the serpent. The result, of course, is the fallen world we live in.

King David was captured by the sight of a woman who was not his wife, and the result was devastating: his family suffered for generations because of his sin (see 2 Samuel 12). David believed the same lie Adam and Eve had believed so long ago in the Garden of Eden: that he could disobey God and everything would work out in the end. As a result, he was taken down by his sin, ensnared and captured by the lust of his heart and a pride that says, "My ways are just as good as God's."

The lure of sin, especially sexual sin, is as powerful and devastating today as it was in King David's time. It's the only sin that the Bible tells us to run from (see 1 Corinthians 6:18). Why? Because God, who made us, knows how we're wired. He knows how difficult it is for human beings to escape sexual sin. Once temptation has turned to transgression, the result is heartbreak unlike any other.

It's easy to slip off the narrow road when it comes to this issue. How often do we entertain thoughts of what God says to run from? How often do we watch things on our private screens because we have squelched the still, small voice of our Creator? If you're like me, I'm guessing quite a few times. We are so easily captured—often by our own complacency.

Tune your heart to His today, precious one. The

war is raging on the battlefield of human sexuality. The world shakes its fist at the Creator God, boldly defying the clear boundaries God has lovingly put in place for our protection. Today I pray that we would declare our unwillingness to be captured by anything and anyone except the One who made us and loves us most. This battle is fierce—but God has made a way.

If you have suffered the devastating effects of being captured by sexual sin, whether through pornography, abuse, or adultery, God says, "Look up! Look to Me!" He offers hope and healing for the captured human heart. The war that rages for rulership of our hearts is no match for the One who sent His Son for those hearts. Cry out to Him. Grace and freedom are yours for the asking. He is the rescue we need.

LORD, HELP ME PROTECT my children's hearts by protecting their eyes.

This is a struggle, because if I look—really look—at what my children see every day, I know I have to start with what I'm allowing myself to see. You say we need to run from sexual sin, and we're so surrounded by it on the battlefield these days that sometimes I don't know if I can ever stop running.

So please let this battle be won first in my heart. I boldly declare that I want to be captured—but only by You.

Let me long for what is pure and true and lovely. I battle with my flesh in this area, Lord, so I know my children must be struggling too.

When I hear Your still, small voice, incline my ears to listen. Don't let me turn away; don't let me tune You out. I realize now that if I don't have victory in this area of my life, my children will suffer.

I know that the enemy of my children's souls is real and that the struggle can't be won without surrender. When we surrender to You, You promise to rescue us from the snare of the enemy. And so I make this bold request in Your name: May I come to my senses and escape the snare of the devil, even though he wants to capture me to do his will.

I pray for the men in my life, Lord. Protect their eyes from seeing things that would cause their hearts to be captured by the siren song of sexual sin. Show me anything in my life that would be a stumbling block—even the little things.

I pray for the women in my life, Lord. Draw our daughters to men who will love them the way You have designed them to be loved, and let them experience Your vision for sex, within the boundaries of a godly marriage. You plan is for our good, Lord. Your design for sex is beautiful. Help us keep it that way in the midst of a culture that denies Your created order.

Lord, thank You for the children You have entrusted to my care. I have so much to be thankful for, and I often forget that. Today, even as I pray for protection against the many things we have access to that we don't want, I thank You for all that we have.

Praying the Scriptures:

1 CORINTHIANS 6:18; PHILIPPIANS 4:8; HEBREWS 13:4

A PRAYER *for the* MOM
of a SPECIAL-NEEDS CHILD

Thank you for making me so wonderfully complex!
Your workmanship is marvelous—how well I know
it. You watched me as I was being formed in utter
seclusion, as I was woven together in the dark of
the womb.

PSALM 139:14-15

From the moment we see a positive sign on a pregnancy
test, dreams about this new life begin to make their
home in our hearts. But we don't always get what we
are expecting. Sometimes we get much, much more.

Early one spring morning I received a call from my
sister. Her voice was frantic with worry. Holly had just
come home from her twenty-two-week prenatal visit.
Like most mothers-to-be, she expected an ordinary
office call: fetal heart tones, measurements, an ultra-
sound. But the news she received that day was anything
but ordinary.

"Heidi?" she began. "The doctor just told me that my baby has Down syndrome. We're supposed to go back for further testing tomorrow." A few weeks earlier, Holly had had a blood test that revealed an elevated alpha-fetoprotein (AFP) level. As a childbirth educator, I knew the high number of false positives with the AFP, so I assured her that everything would be all right. I'd had a few false positives myself. "Nothing to worry about," I said. I was wrong. Now that they'd done an amniocentesis, there was no mistaking the results. The pressure to have an abortion was palpable.

The doctors and genetic counselors knew a lot about baby Kendall's future. They told my sister that if she decided to let her baby live, her little girl would be born with the rarest form of Down syndrome, called translocation. It was a devastating diagnosis. To make matters worse, Kendall was among the approximately half of all infants born with Down syndrome to have a heart defect. In one sixty-minute session, Holly's expectations of what her daughter's life would be like were shattered. The doctors were blunt: Kendall's outlook was grim.

In a culture that would rather abort a baby with a birth defect than protect her, a mother's love must be fierce.

My sister chose life for Kendall that day, and on June 11, 1999, just a few short months after we learned she would be different, she was born. Today Kendall is a young adult. Her life has not been easy, but I can say with certainty that she is the light of my sister's life. When I recently asked Holly about her decision to choose life for her precious special delivery, she reminded me that the life she really saved was her own. "Kendall has taught me what unconditional love looks like. No matter what she is going through, she will always give you a hug and tell you that she loves you. And in the scary moments when she struggles to breathe, her focus is on me. 'Mommy, are you okay?' Kendall has taught me that it's not what you're born with—it's what you do with it that matters."

If you're facing a special delivery, know this: God is with you. He is for you. He will carry you—and your precious child—to destinations marked by grace and joy. Live with courage as you walk this life alongside your special child. Good things are coming!

I HURT FOR THE STRUGGLE my child is facing, Lord. But can I be vulnerable enough to say that I'm hurting for my own struggle too? The dreams I had for my child are not going to come true, so can You give me new dreams? Dreams that will match the season we're in? Can You give me Your dreams for my precious child?

The struggle is real. Financial struggles. Medical bills. Stress. Fear. Help me not to worry about tomorrow. Help me not to be anxious about anything, but in everything, by prayer and supplication with thanksgiving, let my requests be made known to You. I believe that Your peace, which surpasses all understanding, will guard my heart and my mind in Christ Jesus.

I believe You will supply all my needs—and the needs of my child—according to Your riches in Christ Jesus. Please help me to consider it pure joy, even as I face trials of many kinds, knowing that the testing of my faith will develop perseverance.

You say that I will not lack anything—and I believe You! Help my unbelief! Strengthen my resolve to cling to Your promises, and help me remember that You will never take me or my child where Your grace will not sustain us. On the days when we face unexpected challenges, clothe us with your peace. On the days when we are weary, help us to wait on You, mounting up with wings like eagles.

Strengthen the relationships around this special child, Lord. Strengthen our family. Guard our home. Keep our hearts trusting in Your goodness and leaning hard into Your grace.

Lord, I'm casting my cares on You right now, declaring that You will sustain me. I know that You will never let me be shaken. So I stand on Your truth, believing You not only for strength but also for joy on the journey. Thank You for walking this road with me. Thank You for my wonderful, special delivery.

You are good.

Praying the Scriptures:

ISAIAH 41:10; ROMANS 8:31; PHILIPPIANS 4:6-7, 19; JAMES 1:2-4; PSALM 23:1; ISAIAH 40:31; PSALM 55:22

Children are a gift from the LORD;
they are a reward from him.

PSALM 127:3

God knew that I wasn't ready to be pregnant again. I stared at the positive result as I blinked away hot tears. I was tired. Really tired. Knowing how tight our budget was stretched already, we *thought* we'd done everything we could to prevent another pregnancy. If I was honest, though, it wasn't just about the money. It was about me, too. With four children under the age of eight, I had a full plate. I doubted my ability to be the mother to the children I already had! The day I took that pregnancy test—well, let's just say it wasn't exactly a day I was winning at motherhood.

I also wondered what people would think. There was a time when I thought our family was "just right." With two girls and two boys, we fit perfectly into our six-passenger van. Burgerville (our local version of McDonald's) had a comfy corner booth for six where we could go relatively unnoticed as a family. No big deal—not too big, not too small. Culturally correct. No one stared at us. We fit the expected family norm in our town.

My husband's salary was just right too—not too small, but not so large that we forgot to depend on the Lord for all the unexpected things that come to every family. Unexpected mechanic bills. Unexpected company. (Not necessarily in that order.) The challenges we don't expect seem to come up in every area of our lives—emotional, financial, and spiritual. But this unexpected pregnancy seemed like a bigger challenge than we were ready for. Finding out you're pregnant when you feel like your parenting dance card is already full is a little like noticing you're too tired to dance just before the boy you really wanted to dance with asks you to be his partner.

We're too tired for this challenge, yes. But the opportunity to dance brings all manner of unexpected blessings, doesn't it? Each child comes to us fresh from heaven with a unique calling and purpose in life . . . starting with that child's mother. It's almost like God knows what's best for us, right down to those unexpected blessings! (Turns out, God really does know what we need!)

Since we live in a world that doesn't value human

life, we need God's perspective more than ever. In a world that says children are a burden, it's easy to lose sight of the blessing, even unknowingly. But when we exchange our plans for God's plans, when we choose to believe that our children, planned or unplanned, are a blessing, the sure result is joy.

According to the Bible, we make our plans, but the Lord directs our steps (see Proverbs 16:9). He knows what's best for us, and what's more, He works all things together for our good, right down to an unplanned pregnancy. His ways are always, ever, only good.

I WASN'T "READY" for this pregnancy, Lord. I feel caught off guard. I'm trying to trust Your timing, but right now, it feels like the timing isn't right. We haven't budgeted for another baby. Honestly, I'm not sure I can handle more responsibility and be the wife and mother you want me to be. I feel overwhelmed at the thought of another child. I need Your perspective.

I want to see this baby as a gift, the way You talk about in Your Word. I want to feel the joy deep down in my spirit. I know Your plans are good and that this child belongs to You. Thank You for choosing me to be the one to nurture and love this tiny person who is made in Your image.

And since I can't always count on my words, I'm going to say Your words as I pray over this unexpected blessing. I don't know the path of the wind or how the body is formed in my womb, so I can't understand Your work, God. Yet you are the maker of all things, and I trust You. I cast all my cares on You, knowing that You care for me—and for the unborn life I carry inside me.

Lord, please give me strength when I am weary, joy as I announce this new life, and peace as I process how this baby will change the life I know. You said I can do all things through Christ who gives me strength, so I know You will give me the strength I need to carry this precious child until the day I give birth and beyond.

Thank You for all you have given to me. Thank You for this new life inside me. As I balance all that You have entrusted to me, help me to make time to renew my spirit and restore my body. Give me the strength to love my family well.

You know this child as they are still in the womb, even before they're born, just as You knew the prophet Jeremiah. You are the author of life, and I praise You because this baby is fearfully and wonderfully made. Your works are wonderful, including this baby, and my soul knows it full well.

Praying the Scriptures:

PROVERBS 16:9; PSALM 127; ECCLESIASTES 11:5; 1 PETER 5:7; ISAIAH 40:31; PHILIPPIANS 4:13; JEREMIAH 1:5; PSALM 139

> My son, keep your father's commandment, and
> forsake not your mother's teaching. Bind them on
> your heart always; tie them around your neck.

PROVERBS 6:20-21, ESV

*P*arenting is faith work at every stage, whether we're sending our kids off to kindergarten or to college. We have no assurance of how things will turn out as we let go of our children, but we do have the assurance that God will never leave or forsake us. As our children leave home, this knowledge takes on new significance.

When our children were young, this idea of releasing our children into the world sounded easy enough to my husband, Jay, and me. But as they started to move toward independence, we began to learn something new: we had to depend on the Lord in a new way.

If you're feeling the strange mixture of sadness and worry along with the joy and excitement that comes from watching your children pursue their dreams—if your arrow is almost ready to fly—be encouraged. God is saying, "You still need Me on this parenting journey! I'm still here!"

Jay and I have noticed that as our children get older, they leave the physical borders of our home, but they never leave the spiritual boundaries of our prayers. In fact, the breadth and depth of our prayers grow as our children grow. If we don't tremble at the responsibility we have as parents of emerging adults, I think we may be misunderstanding our role. If we don't tremble, we may not understand the magnitude of the spiritual battle we engaged in the moment we became parents.

So tremble, but keep trusting. If we tremble to the point of faithless worry, we have forgotten who we serve.

Jim Elliot, who became famous after being martyred as a missionary to a native tribe in Ecuador, wrote this to his parents after telling them his plans:

Remember how the Psalmist described children? He said that they were as an heritage from the Lord, and that every man should be happy who had his quiver full of them. And what is a quiver full of but arrows?

And what are arrows for but to shoot? So, with the strong arms of prayer, draw the bowstring back and let the arrows fly—all of them, straight at the Enemy's hosts.[1]

I love how tender Jim's heart was toward his parents. His words continue to bless me as my kids grow and leave the nest that we have spent a lifetime feathering. Just as Jim gently reminded his parents that their job was to release him to God's Kingdom purpose for his life, let's encourage each other in the big picture of parenting. The big picture is this: our children are arrows intended to serve the Lord of heaven's armies. Our children are not ours at all; they are on loan to us, given to us from our gracious, good Father.

If it's time to launch your arrow, and if you can feel your palms sweat and your arms shake, take heart. The Lord will be with your arrow in the same way He has been with you. Our God-given mandate as parents is clear: we are to love and train our children in God's truth—so we can release them to God's eternal purposes.

LORD, YOU SAY MY CHILDREN are given to me as arrows, but sometimes I doubt my archery abilities are strong enough for such a

---

[1] Elisabeth Elliot, *Shadow of the Almighty* (New York: Harper Collins, 1958), 132.

precious launch. Would You steady my stance as I raise my bow high and draw back the bowstring? This prayer is as much for me as it is for my arrow-child. We both need You. Keep my arrow close to You, Lord.

Sometimes I feel the accuser's hot breath on my neck. I am reminded of my failures, of words I said that I can't take back, of missed opportunities, of times I didn't set the example You wanted me to set. Would You focus my eyes on You? Would You silence the voice of my enemy and instead tune my ears to the gentle leading of Your Spirit?

I want to be like You, Lord—in part because I want to be obedient, but also because I want my children to follow me as I follow Christ. Help me to follow You in every area of my life. Help me to teach my children that the only way to keep their lives pure is to live according to Your Word.

Scripture says that we are to train ourselves for godliness. My time to train my warrior-child is coming to a close, but please help me to continue to train my own heart and mind so I can be the woman You created me to be. Please give me opportunities to speak into the lives of my children. Show me how I can be a godly influence for them, even as they become adults. You are good at multiplying. Like the loaves and fishes, will You take the moments I have with my children and multiply them in power?

Surround my grown children with godly people, from professors to mentors to friends. As I release these arrows into the world, I pray that You will guide and direct the path ahead. I pray that my children will love Your Word and desire to follow You in every area of life.

And Lord, I pray for blessing—blessing so rich that they can't deny it's the result of the move of Your hand. Please bless my children with a heart that seeks after righteousness. May their relationships draw them closer to You.

Thank You that You have a plan for my children—a plan for good and not harm. Thank You that You never slumber or sleep and that Your eyes are always on my children. Steady my heart, Lord, and deepen my dependence on You as I let my—Your—precious arrows fly.

Praying the Scriptures:

Isaiah 52:7; Matthew 28:19-20; 1 Timothy 4:7; Deuteronomy 6:6-7, 9; Psalm 119:9; Jeremiah 29:11; Psalm 121:4

WISDOM *for the* BATTLEFIELD

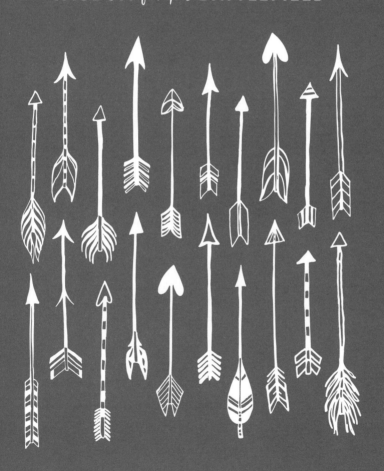

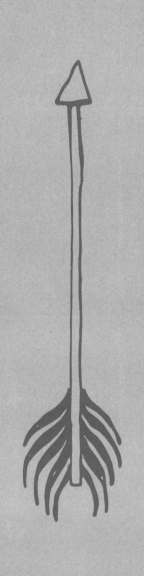

A PRAYER *for* MY CHILD'S TEACHER

The student is not above the teacher, but everyone who is fully trained will be like their teacher.

LUKE 6:40, NIV

*P*eople sometimes ask me why I homeschool. Honestly? As the mother of seven children, I ask myself sometimes too. I always considered myself an unlikely candidate for mothering, and I can assure you, homeschooling was around negative twenty on my list of things I wanted to do after I became a mother. After all, why would a woman choose to bypass the (free) public education system and instead decide to take full responsibility for the education of her children?

It's a good question. But before we take sides about whether homeschooling is the right answer for your family or mine, let's make sure we understand the deeper issue. Keep in mind, we are on a battlefield. We have a real enemy, and we're in a real war. Much is at stake. So rather than getting hung up on styles of education—public school or private school or home-schooling, a classical education model or a Charlotte Mason approach, let's look at parenting and education through the lens of Scripture.

The Bible says that parents are responsible for the training of their children. In Deuteronomy 6, right after the command to love the Lord with all our heart, soul, and strength, we are instructed to impress God's commandments on our children. Then Scripture takes it even further, giving parents specific instructions about when this impressing is to be done.

> You must commit yourselves wholeheartedly
> to these commands that I am giving you today.
> Repeat them again and again to your children.
> Talk about them when you are at home and
> when you are on the road, when you are going
> to bed and when you are getting up.
>
> DEUTERONOMY 6:6-7

When I read this passage, I thought, *That's pretty much all day!* But it doesn't seem like a command to a particular kind of education. Instead, it's a clear teaching on what a parent's first priority should be: to train our children in God's ways—and at the very least, to know who else is teaching our children.

In Luke 6:40, we get to the heart of why education is such a major part of the battle for the hearts and minds of our kids:

> The student is not above the teacher, but everyone who is fully trained will be like their teacher. (NIV)

Who is my child's teacher? The obvious answer is *me* (whether I homeschool or not), because I am my child's first teacher. "The apple," as the old saying goes, "doesn't fall far from the tree." We are responsible for making sure the example we set for our children is a godly one. But we don't do this thing called life in a vacuum. According to the Bible, everyone who is fully trained will be "like their teacher." Everyone.

If we believe what God says about students and teachers is true, then it's time to get serious about education. Education, by its very nature, is not neutral. The *how* of education is important, but according to God's Word, an even more important component is the *who*. So whatever educational decisions you make for your children, remember that ultimately you are your children's first and most important teacher, and you are the one who will influence them most when it comes to training them in the ways of the Lord.

Remember, our common enemy wants us divided

about educational choices, but God is interested in much more than that. God is after our hearts—starting with parents.

YOUR WORD SAYS my children will be like their teacher, Lord.

Today I realize that *I am that teacher*. Would You show me how to become the person You want me to be so that my children can become who You want them to be too? Help me to love You with all my heart, soul, and strength. Help me to remember the commands You have given so I can teach them to my children. Help me to take advantage of every opportunity to teach Your ways to my children, from the time we get up to the time we go to bed.

I also see that everyone who influences my children matters. Help me to see influence as something that carries eternal consequences and to act in the best spiritual interest of my child on the battlefield of education. Give me insight into the hearts and motives of those who carry influence with my children. Open my eyes to wrong teaching, wrong motives, and a worldview that opposes You, so I can make sure my children learn what is right according to Your standard, not the world's.

You say that the person who doesn't sit in the counsel of the wicked will be blessed. In this crazy world, it's sometimes hard to tell the wicked from the righteous! Snares are everywhere, including on the battlefield of education. You say that if anyone lacks wisdom, they can ask You for it, so I'm asking. Please give me—and my children— daily wisdom in discerning good from evil.

I pray for my child's teacher, Lord—starting with me. Help me to be an instructor who brings life and truth—Your life, Your truth—to the heart of my children's education, no matter the subject.

Praying the Scriptures:

Deuteronomy 6:1-25; Proverbs 1:7;
Proverbs 22:6; Psalm 1; James 1:5

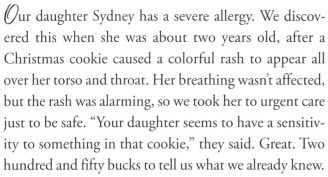

Guard your heart above all else,
for it determines the course of your life.

PROVERBS 4:23

*O*ur daughter Sydney has a severe allergy. We discovered this when she was about two years old, after a Christmas cookie caused a colorful rash to appear all over her torso and throat. Her breathing wasn't affected, but the rash was alarming, so we took her to urgent care just to be safe. "Your daughter seems to have a sensitivity to something in that cookie," they said. Great. Two hundred and fifty bucks to tell us what we already knew.

The trouble was, there were a lot of things in the cookie. We'd never seen her react to food before. Was it the food coloring? The pecans? The gluten? No one knew for sure, but the doctor issued a "play it safe" warning as we left the office that evening. "Her first reaction may be just the beginning," he said. "She might have a more serious reaction if she's exposed again. Watch what she eats. The reaction time gets faster as the allergy progresses."

Listen. When you have seven children, it's a lot of work (not to mention nearly impossible) to watch everything each child is eating. Until you know how high the stakes are, that is.

At first we didn't take the warning too seriously. I mean, really, how bad could it get? As you might have guessed, however, my lazy, complacent approach to Syd's allergy backfired. Two months later, she reacted to a single bite of caramel-pecan ice cream. Within five minutes of ingesting the ice cream, her entire body was covered in hives. A few minutes later, she began throwing up while struggling to breathe. She was in trouble.

Fortunately, we lived just two minutes from a major hospital. I called them as we were pulling out of our driveway, and a medical team met us in the parking lot, where she was given oxygen and a shot of epinephrine. That shot saved her life. Suddenly, the $250 we paid for the initial warning seemed like pocket change. We would have paid $250 million to save her life. I was willing to do whatever work it took to keep this from happening again. Just one major reaction was enough to teach us a very powerful lesson: warnings matter.

All through the Word of God, we are warned of the spiritual implications of not guarding our hearts.

Solomon says that our hearts set the course for our entire life—they are something worth protecting, something valuable. Notice that Solomon makes a pretty sweeping statement in this exhortation. He says the heart is worth guarding "above all else." *Bam.*

Your heart is the source of everything you do. The thoughts and intentions of the heart flow into words, words flow into actions, and actions flow into life-altering consequences. If your heart is unhealthy, it will affect everything around you—your marriage, your parenting, your career, your ministry, and even your legacy. (Just ask Solomon about that.) Our children are greatly affected by our decision to guard our hearts (or our decision not to). We must guard ourselves against sin, wrong priorities, and even our desire to direct our own lives.

Don't let laziness turn your legacy into a liability. Don't wait until you're on your way to the spiritual emergency room to decide that your heart is worth protecting.

I DON'T WANT TO BE lazy about protecting my heart, Lord.

I know that I need to be fully invested in winning the battle to appreciate why I need to guard my heart, but I confess that I often don't want to do the work. It's easier to assume that I can read my Bible occasionally and pray when things get too difficult to manage. It just seems easier. I have plenty of excuses for not strengthening the wall around my heart: the kids kept me up late, work is pressing, I'm tired.

But as I study Your Word, I know that this guarding isn't something I can be passive about. Solomon says that a lazy person is smarter in his own eyes than seven wise counselors. I recognize in his description the defensive posture of a person who knows better but just doesn't want to do it. Help me to come to terms with the status of my heart and what I need to do to protect it.

Father, I can think of so many areas where my heart needs guarding. I want Your joy and peace to reign in my heart, but more often than not, I struggle to make headway as I feel around for Your path. The road often seems foggy and dark.

Help me to discern the voice of the enemy, especially where guarding my heart is concerned. Satan would have me believe that my heart isn't worth protecting—after all, it's often troubled, grieved, burdened, and even broken. But Lord, I know that You came to heal bruised hearts like mine.

Help me to set an example for my children by walking in right relationship with You. Help me to learn to walk with You moment by moment—not just by reading my Bible and praying, but by constantly living in Your presence. Help me to always be aware of Your commands, Your purpose for my life, and my dependence on You.

I don't want to grow complacent about my walk with You. I know that the only way I can model a life of faithfulness is through Your strength, so please help me to not grow weary in doing good. I long to hear You say, "Well done, good and faithful servant!"

Guard my heart, Lord, that I might not sin against You, and let me experience the joy of keeping Your commands. Help me to remain in Your love and to pass that love to my children with joy.

Praying the Scriptures:

PROVERBS 4:20-27; PROVERBS 26:16; JOHN 15:10-17

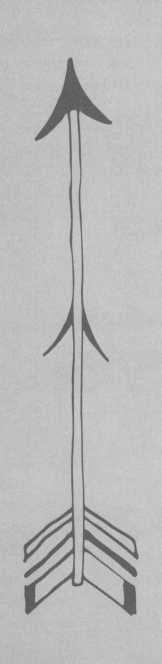

OBEDIENCE = BLESSING

A PRAYER *for the* MOM WHO
LONGS *to* SEE *beyond the* BATTLE

> We know that for those who love God all things work
> together for good, for those who are called according
> to his purpose.

ROMANS 8:28, ESV

It's easy to lose sight of the big story (God's story) when
we're mired down in the day-to-day of parenting. The
mundane tasks that make up the sometimes long days of
motherhood can cloud our view. We're easily sidetracked
and discouraged. But God wants us to remember that He
is still at work. He is doing something much bigger than we
can see, especially when life is difficult and the battle is long.

No one understood long battles like the Israelites.

The priest Ezra, who lived in Israel in the fifth century
BC, was born in God's perfect timing—onto the battlefield
of a lifetime. He has something to teach us about God's
unfailing promise, even in the face of our own rebellion.

In the book of Ezra, we find a historical record that

links two important time periods for the Israelite people: the era that directly followed the seventy years they were held in Babylonian captivity and the era when they became apathetic and lazy (again).

The book of Ezra tells the epic story of a dethroned king, a captured people, and the death of Judah as an independent nation. But even more than that, it provides an account of the regathering of the Jews and their struggle to rebuild what was lost though their disobedience. Through it all, Ezra boldly declares that God has not forgotten His people.

Through Ezra's account, we witness the rebuilding of the Temple and the unification of the returning tribes. The people worked together to achieve the common purpose of seeing the Temple restored, but eventually—like all of us—they grew weary. When weariness settled in, apathy wasn't far behind, and the people stopped their rebuilding work. That's when Ezra showed up on the scene with two thousand reinforcements, and his obedience resulted in spiritual revival. By the end of the book, Israel is restored to God, having repented and renewed their covenant, and then acting on that covenant through obedience to God.

The Israelites in Ezra's day weren't that different from my own family and me, come to think of it. We struggle every day to achieve the goal of growing in Christ. Scratch that—we struggle just to get along. Growing in Christ seems to happen only after months and years of three steps forward and two steps back. Can you relate? If so, take heart. We may feel discouraged, but God is still at work!

Listen to one of the great intercessory prayers of the Bible:

> O LORD, God of Israel, you are just. We come before you in our guilt as nothing but an escaped remnant, though in such a condition none of us can stand in your presence.
>
> EZRA 9:15

Ezra didn't want the people to lose sight of their place in the grand scheme of God's great story. They were a disobedient, escaped remnant, unworthy to stand in God's presence. Yet God gave them grace. Does this sound familiar?

If you are facing an uncompleted construction project in your heart today, look up! Don't allow the enemy to drag your spirit into the swamp of apathy and disobedience. Ask God to renew your vision by giving you a glimpse into His. When we see things from God's perspective, our lives are changed forever. God is always at work. He won't forget His promises.

THE UNFINISHED WORK around me is obscuring my eternal view today, Father.

I feel like the work I'm doing with my children isn't yielding much (if any) fruit. One day I feel I'm making progress, and then I'll have a day (or a series of them) that makes me wonder if that "progress" was just an illusion. I'm tempted to give up, to stop the constant instruction and correction.

Forgive me for forgetting that You are always at work. Forgive me for being so focused on what isn't happening that I forget what *is* happening. I know You are at work in the tiny steps my children are taking, both physically and spiritually. I see Your hand in my life as my desire to know You grows. Thank You for helping me to see past the construction hazards—past the laundry and the dishes and the homework and the struggle to connect with a strong-willed toddler or a moody teen.

Lord, please remove any obstacles to my spiritual growth—even if that obstacle is my own stubbornness. Like Ezra, I want to see my sin for what it is: a barrier to Your blessing.

You said that those who love You keep Your commandments. Well, I love You, Father, and I want my life to show it. I want Your blessing, God—in my family, in my community, in my church, and in our nation. Help us to follow You in a way that pleases You and brings glory to Your name. In Your unfailing love, don't abandon us—bring us back to You. Remind us that Your Word is true and that those who trust in You and obey You are blessed.

Praying the Scriptures:

Ezra 9:5-15; John 14:15

RUN HIM OFF!

A PRAYER *for the* MOM WHO FEELS POWERLESS

Submit therefore to God.
Resist the devil and he will flee from you.

JAMES 4:7, NASB

From the beginning of time, the devil has sought to rob God's children of the good things God has planned. If we allow him to take the upper hand, he'll take it. But we sometimes forget this important fact: the devil is no match for God. Satan has no authority over God or God's people. My grandma used to say, "The devil doesn't have permission to be on your property! Run him off!"

Grandma knew—she wasn't afraid. And she used her influence in my life to teach me that God's power is greater than any force on heaven or earth. When Grandma said, "Run him off!" it wasn't something she said lightly. It was the result of years of warfare. She knew what all Christians need to know: Satan has no authority over God's people. There is no comparison between our powerful God and the god of this world. Satan is a created being; God is infinite.

So how do we get the upper hand with the devil? We start by understanding the limited power he has. Yes, Satan afflicts believers, and we shouldn't underestimate him. Satan is the god of this world, and the Bible says that unbelievers are under his power, blinded by their sin. But we shouldn't give him more credit than he deserves. Satan is powerful, but he's not all-powerful. Christ will have ultimate victory over Satan, and that means those of us who are in Christ will have ultimate victory over him too.

Christian mom, know whose you are. You belong to God. And your children need to know that the moment they accept Jesus Christ into their lives, they belong to God too. Satan can't do anything without God's permission. It's true that Satan was the wicked force behind Job's suffering, but Satan had to ask permission from God for every single thing he did. This is a clear reminder: Satan can do only what God allows. When God allows Satan to afflict one of His own, you can trust that it's for a Kingdom purpose. God wants us to display His power and glory, even through suffering, so that others may come to know the hope we have in Christ.

Satan works to discredit the work of God in our lives,

but God wants us to bear witness to His saving grace and His power over sin. We are more than conquerors through Him who loves us! Because of the sacrifice of Jesus, we are no longer slaves to sin. Because of His work, we share in the victory Jesus won at the Cross.

There's good news, warrior mom! Because Christ has been given all authority over Satan, we can have victory over every struggle we face. Christ's victory means that we can have victory too. The battle is no match for the Lord of heaven's armies. He is destined to be victorious!

THANK YOU, LORD, for the victory You have secured over Satan and sin. Thank You that because of the sacrifice of Jesus, I don't have to be a slave to sin any longer. Thank You for forgiveness in Jesus!

Sometimes I forget that You have already completed the work of forgiveness on my behalf, and I am tempted to doubt Your character. When I'm tempted, please remind me that the temptation isn't from You, for You can't be tempted by evil, and You don't tempt anyone. Give me strength to submit myself to You alone. I trust that Your Word is true and that when I resist the devil, he will flee from me because I am Yours.

Father, I come into Your presence with holy wonder. Your power is beyond my imagining, Your grace is beyond my understanding, and Your love is the most powerful force in all of creation. Help me to not live in fear of an enemy You have already defeated.

There are places in my life where I have allowed the devil to tempt me and even rule over me. At times, I forget that You are bigger than the devil, and I make him bigger in my mind than he is. Please enable me to stand firm against the schemes of the evil one. Help me to put on Your full armor so that I can take my stand against any scheme of the devil.

Help me to trust Your heart, Lord, even in my suffering. Hold me close when the fighting is fierce, even as I hold my children close. I want to paint a picture of Your greatness for my children to see, and I know that they see the picture primarily in the way I live my life.

So, Father, I pray that my life would be lived to bring glory to You—to reflect Your majesty, Your love, Your power, Your forgiveness, Your hope, and Your healing. You have not left me alone in this battle against the evil one. You have equipped me with the belt of truth, the breastplate of righteousness, the shield of faith, the helmet of salvation, and the sword of the Spirit. Help me to put on the full armor of God so that I can stand firm against the schemes of the devil.

I lift up my eyes to the hills, knowing that my help comes from You.

Praying the Scriptures:

2 Corinthians 12:7-10; Romans 8:37; Romans 6:16-18; James 1:13; 4:7; Ephesians 6:10-18; 1 Peter 5:8-9; Psalm 121

A PRAYER *for the* MOM
WHO NEEDS *a* WIN

Greater is he that is in you than
he that is in the world.

1 JOHN 4:4, ASV

One thing that must break the heart of God is how many of us Christians live our lives without truly knowing the power that is available to us through the shed blood of Jesus. It's like being unnecessarily exposed to radiation only because you didn't know there was a way to avoid it or like living in a tiny prison cell even though the door was unlocked. For all our talk of spiritual battles, I wonder: Do we know how to live into the authority God has given us through Christ?

By living into something, I mean leaning hard, resting in it without being afraid that the thing you're leaning on will give way. You can't lean hard into something unless you trust that it's going to hold you up. When we truly understand that it is God, not us, who is fighting on this battlefield, we can lean on Christ and find rest in the middle of even the fiercest battle.

But how do we engage an adversary as powerful and formidable as Satan? We start with a plan. For goodness' sake, every successful day needs a plan, right? Whenever I head into my day without a plan, I end up one of two things: disappointed or defeated. It's no fun to make it to the end of the day and feel the sting of regret. The same is true in our battle with the enemy of our souls. As Christians, we've been given the ultimate battle plan: to engage our enemy in the name of God's Son, Jesus. Even better, we're guaranteed victory in His name.

While it's true that we're assured the victory, we are sure to experience times of testing. If we want the testimony that comes after the test is over, we need to have a strategy in place. Are you walking through a valley? Is your child struggling with temptation or sin? Come before the Lord in prayer, and arm yourself daily with these strategies for spiritual warfare, using the acronym VICTORY:

Vigilantly keep watch. Recognize that we have a powerful adversary who should not be underestimated (see 1 Peter 5:8).

Insist on praise. Praising God is like kryptonite to the devil. No matter what happens, affirm the goodness of God (see James 1:2-4).

Claim the higher ground. Stay on the narrow road, and do what's right (see Galatians 6:9).

Take up the armor of God. It's not enough to know what the armor is; we must put it on through prayer each day (see Ephesians 6).

Own your own sin. We will never be victorious if we are harboring unconfessed sin (see 2 Corinthians 7:9-10).

Rest in the goodness of God's plan. He is always, ever, only good (see Psalm 145:9).

Yield your will. Just like children must yield to their parents' loving discipline, we yield to God's correction (see John 14:23).

FATHER, I want to walk in the authority of Your Son. I want to show my children what true victory looks like.

I recognize that I can't do this apart from the empowerment and conviction of the Holy Spirit. I need You to teach me how to walk in Your strength instead of my own. The battle is real, but You are bigger than any force of evil in this world.

Most of the time the attacks and struggles that come my way don't cause me to praise You. To be honest, I'm more prone to panic. Praise isn't something that comes naturally to me in the midst of a challenge, and yet it's something I need to learn. Sometimes the water is deep. Sometimes my feet don't touch the spiritual ground under my feet, and my faith flounders. So Lord, I'm counting on You to remind me that when the days are long and the finances are tight and the struggle is more real than I want it to be, those are the times I need to praise You most.

This daily struggle with sin brings me to my knees. Lord, help me to own my sin, and give me the courage to confront the sin I see in my children. Help me to identify with their struggle instead of excusing it so that we can all learn—my children and me—about the rest that comes from walking in the center of Your will. Lower the defenses of my heart so that I can raise a righteous defense against the enemy of my soul.

Lord, as I consider the battlefield and the many snares that litter its landscape, I pray for eyes to see the direction You want me to go and a heart to embrace Your instruction. Teach me to lean into Your will with a joyful obedience that demonstrates my love for You and Your Word. After all, I know that true victory can only come through obedience to You.

I pray for obedience and victory for my children, too. It seems that I ask my children to obey me several times each day, and I am often met with steely disobedience or, at the very least, the threat of it. Now, as I come before You, I see that I struggle to obey You, my heavenly Father. But You consistently see me through Your eyes of grace. Please give me grace for my children, even as You extend grace to me.

Lord, let my eyes look straight ahead; fix my gaze on You. Cause me to give careful thought to the paths I take, and keep me steadfast in all my ways. I am trusting that Your grace will carry my children and me to victory, one day, one decision, at a time.

Praying the Scriptures:

Exodus 14:13-14; 1 Corinthians 15:57; 1 John 2:3-6; Isaiah 48:17-19; Luke 11:28; Proverbs 4:25-27

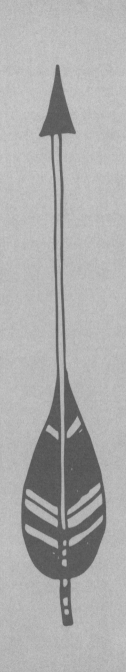

WEAPONS *for the* BATTLEFIELD

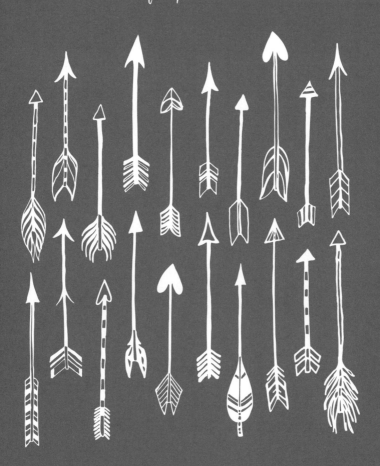

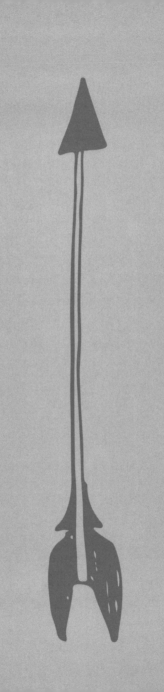

> Your word is a lamp to guide my feet
> and a light for my path.
>
> PSALM 119:105

*H*ave you ever been in true darkness? Scientists define darkness as the total absence of light—something that's rare in the developed world because we have so many sources of artificial light. If you've ever been out in the Alaskan tundra in the middle of the night, you've gotten a glimpse of true darkness. You'll know when you've seen it because the stars appear brighter than they do in the city. They're not brighter, of course, but the contrast is clearer when the light pierces the darkness.

Light and darkness stand in stark opposition to each other. In the spiritual realm, darkness isn't something to play around with; it's deadly (see 1 John 1:5-6). The good news is that we don't have to stay in spiritual darkness—God has given us the light of His Word.

You would think that one look around the world today would motivate us to learn God's Word, but so often we choose to stay in darkness simply out of indifference or laziness.

Few things are more alarming in the church today than our lack of biblical literacy. Even though we have multiple versions of the Bible and countless study materials at our fingertips, we often ignore this weapon that combats the darkness all around us.

As a result, we have become an easy target. Our great adversary, the devil, is preying on a generation of biblically illiterate Christians—men and women who claim the name of Jesus but don't know His Word and can't defend it. If that sounds like a daunting reality, it is. But we have the ability to turn the tide of biblical illiteracy in our generation and for generations to come. This turnaround starts with a commitment to knowing the Bible.

There are many ways we can absorb God's Word. The easiest way is through hearing it. Thanks to the Internet and phone apps, we can quickly begin listening to the Word.

The next way to get God's Word into our hearts is by reading it. This requires commitment, but I'm here to tell you, precious mom, that your commitment to reading your Bible daily will pay eternal dividends. When we get serious about reading God's Word, our eyes begin to open to our own sin, and we become more effective in every area of our lives, from our relationship with God to our relationships with others.

Another way to combat biblical illiteracy is to study the Bible and commit verses to memory. When God's Word is planted deep inside, God can use it to convict us of sin and wake us up to the dangers of disobedience. Modern technology has made it easier than ever to study the Bible. We can follow good teachers, download Bible study materials, and even start online Bible studies with friends and family.

If we're going to be successful in our battle for the hearts and minds of our children, and if we're going to teach them how to fight this battle successfully, we need to know the Bible. This is not optional for the believer. God knew that we would need a lamp for our feet and a light for our path, so He gave us just such a light in His Word.

Know Your Bible, precious mom! The Bible contains all the light you need to navigate this dark world effectively. Show the enemy you mean business: read and know God's Word.

YOUR WORD IS PRECIOUS TO ME, FATHER.

Thank You that every word it contains is true. Thank You that I can gain wisdom through the Bible and through the power of Your Spirit. I believe that all Scripture is inspired by You and is useful for correcting, preparing, and training me so that I will be equipped to do every good work You have in store for me.

Lord, Your people are struggling today. There is false teaching, even in the church. We sometimes exchange Your truth for the world's "truth," which isn't truth at all. Would You help me to teach my children the difference between worldly wisdom and Your wisdom? Your words aren't just idle words—they are my life, and they contain life!

I want to long after You as the deer pants for streams of water, and I want my children to long for the living water of Your Word too. Help me to lead my children to Your Word every day, offering them a cool drink from the Bible. Help me to make our times in Your Word a priority, and help those times to be refreshing so that my kids will look forward to our daily time together with You.

The culture is shifting, God. The world doesn't value what You value. We need Your guidance now more than ever. I pray that my family would be like a tree planted by the water that sends its roots toward the stream. I pray we won't need to fear when heat comes or worry in a year of drought, and that we'll never fail to bear fruit.

I know this is what it looks like to follow Your Word and apply it to our lives, but Father, I struggle to make the time to be with You. Slow us down, Lord. Quiet our hearts and focus our eyes on You. We can't see truth without You.

Lord, help me to study and know Your Word. Help me to be sensitive to Your leading as You open my eyes to my sins and shortcomings.

Help me to hide Your Word in my heart, that I might not sin against You. I want Your Word to penetrate my heart so I can be used by You, first in the lives of my children and then in a world in desperate need of a Savior. Let Your light shine brightly through me.

Praying the Scriptures:

1 John 1:5-6; Psalm 119:97-106; 2 Timothy 3:16-17; Deuteronomy 32:47; Psalm 42:1-2; Jeremiah 17:8; Psalm 119:11

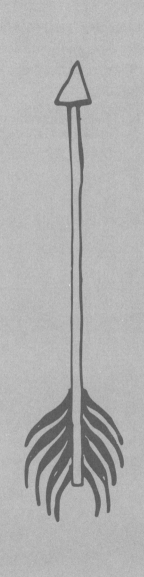

THE WARRIOR'S WEAPON

A PRAYER *for the* MOM
WHO NEEDS *a* GOOD OFFENSE

> Three times a day he got down on his knees and prayed, giving thanks to his God, just as he had done before.

DANIEL 6:10

Nothing will drive you to your knees like motherhood.

Mothers know that the kind of love that pushes our boundaries stretches faith tight. Of course, we've been given this soul-altering love by the author of love Himself. We don't have to get far along on this journey before we discover that motherhood is a lifelong process of applying that love. We learn it in the up-all-night season with newborns and in unexpected trips to the ER and in the agony of waiting for the return of a wandering child.

As the boundaries of our hearts expand, we realize how much we need to come before our heavenly Father. Prayer is where we find comfort, where we pour our hearts out before the One who made us, and where we are reminded how big God is and how small we are.

Prayer is an engagement with the Almighty— an audience with the Creator, a chance to hear from the One who made us and who knows our hurts and unspoken sorrows. He holds the power of life and death in His hands, and He has invited you, precious mom, to come into His presence. We can lay ourselves at His feet, saying, "I can't do this without You."

I have never found a more powerful way to approach the Father than through praying Scripture. This is especially true when the valley is deep and words fall short. Scripture will never fail you, beloved. I am practically out of my chair right now as I say this to you: *When you can't find the words, the living Word can.* Where human words fail, God's Word never will.

Jesus Himself was passionate about the Word of God. He knew how powerful it is for the purpose of intercession. In fact, the Bible says that the devil had to leave Jesus because of the power of the spoken Word of God (see Matthew 4:10-11).

Praying Scripture means taking one of the best weapons of spiritual warfare (prayer) and applying it at twice its strength by using God's own words. It's a one-two knockout punch against the enemy. God's Word brings life.

Learning to pray like Daniel, Esther, or David brings spiritual breakthrough. Just as these three warriors of old discovered, breakthroughs don't happen in the shallows. They happen in the deep places.

What brings you to the end of yourself? What has made your heart so aware of its need that you run to God and fall at His feet? Those are the times of rich communion with Him—when we recognize our need for Him and earnestly seek His comfort, His healing, His presence, and His power.

This mystery of praying Scripture is not so mysterious after all. Simply tell God what He says in His Word. God loves it when we agree with His Word in prayer. When we do, we are uniting with God in the most profound yet simple way. Praying Scripture is life changing not only for you but for your children as well.

I LONG FOR A DEEPER WALK WITH YOU, LORD.

Teach me to pray like Jesus did. He didn't go to You last—He sought You first. I long to get alone with you the way Jesus did, but I'm constantly surrounded by people and responsibility and the pressure to do more.

I know that pride sometimes keeps me from making prayer a priority. I think I'm indispensable and I have to be everywhere and do everything that comes my way. I confess this, and I ask You to forgive me for thinking I can do this life apart from Your wisdom and power. I long to know You the way David did, asking, "When can I go meet with God?"

Draw me close to You, Lord. Help me to recognize the power of prayer so I can be a force for Your Kingdom. I want to come to You like Daniel did: three times a day, he got down on his knees and prayed, giving thanks to You.

When I'm surrounded by hardship and difficulty, I want to be like Esther. She prayed from her weakness, recognizing her need for You. I have no help but You, God. You are my refuge and strength, an ever-present help in time of trouble.

I know that Your thoughts are not like mine and Your ways are not my ways. Father, I pray that You would guard me against making a decision that's contrary to Your Word. Please make my heart inclined to fear You so that things will go well for me and my children.

This world is filled with so much pain, Lord. I often feel inadequate to the task of mothering my children. But I take comfort, boldness, and strength from being alone with You. Thank You that You promise to lead the blind by ways we haven't known, to guide us along unfamiliar paths. Thank You for turning the darkness into light before me and making the rough places smooth.

God, I trust You in times of struggle and success. Make me sensitive to Your Spirit, and help my children to be drawn to You. I long for them to develop their own prayer life—and I know this starts with my example.

I love You, Father, and I love Your Word.

Praying the Scriptures:

MATTHEW 4:10-11; PSALM 42:2; DANIEL 6:10; ESTHER 4; PSALM 46:1; ISAIAH 55:8-9; DEUTERONOMY 5:29; ISAIAH 42:16; JAMES 1; 5:13-20

Just as you received Christ Jesus as Lord,
continue to live your lives in him.

COLOSSIANS 2:6, NIV

I have been privileged to speak before many different groups of people, but my favorite crowd to speak to is influencers. Parents, police officers, politicians, teachers, judges, entrepreneurs, missionaries—all of these influencers carry tremendous force.

Influencers possess a currency that's more powerful than money. Influence means to have an effect on the character, development, or behavior of someone else. That's powerful stuff!

The first influencer in a child's life is their first relationship: their parents. Think back to what shaped you as a young person. Most of us would agree that, for better or worse, our primary influence was our parents. As mothers, we've been given an opportunity to shape the hearts and minds of the next generation. Mothers are called to be a godly influence, training our children in the ways of the Lord. We can't do that without living lives of integrity.

Have you noticed that the devil loves to plague Christians in positions of influence? I would argue that there is nothing more damaging to the cause of Christ than when a person who claims the name of Jesus is exposed for their sinful, selfish behavior. I often think of my own private struggles with my flesh, and while they may not be the kind that make headlines, the Bible teaches that all sin leads to death (see Romans 6:23).

The trouble begins when we engage in what we might consider to be "benign" sin. No one ever plans to become addicted to pornography, have an affair, or become an alcoholic. These "big" sins usually start with small compromises and end up causing us to spiral downward further than we ever imagined. Our enemy is playing for keeps when it comes to personal integrity, and his reasoning is obvious: take out a shepherd, and the wolves have a clean shot at the flock. Take out a Christian in politics, and the name of Christ becomes the target of disdain and contempt. Take out a marriage (and he will use any means necessary), and a family becomes another casualty of spiritual war, leaving the children bewildered and unprotected until the family can find healing and restoration.

Protecting yourself and your children should be at the top of your list of responsibilities as a mother. But there's even more at stake when it comes to living with integrity than receiving the blessing of God. A woman who lives a life of integrity will end up with a powerful currency: godly influence.

What we do in secret matters.

LORD, I KNOW I CAN'T GIVE my children what I don't have.

But I'm struggling in the private spaces of my life. I'm convicted that there are things that don't bother me like they should—"ordinary" sins like watching things I shouldn't watch and engaging in conversations I know don't please You.

Help me to live a life of private integrity so that I can become a woman of godly influence. Help me to be mindful of my role on the battlefield. I don't want to be dragged off and enticed by my own evil desires. Make my spirit keenly aware when I am grieving Your Spirit, Lord.

Thank You that You are my high priest who is able to sympathize with my weaknesses. I'm so grateful that You know what it's like to be temped in every way, just as I am—yet You're without sin.

Help me to steer clear of things that cause me to wander off the path. Remind me that my children are watching—and that as I train them in righteousness, I need to be walking in righteousness too. Keep Your Word before my eyes, Father. As I reflect on Your Word, would You bring to mind the verses that will guard my heart? I know

I'm Your ambassador, Lord. When I sin, help me to confess to You, knowing that You are faithful and just to forgive me and cleanse me from all wickedness.

I want to throw off everything that hinders my walk with You so that I can be an effective warrior. If something I am doing right now is keeping me from being a godly influence in the lives of my children, please open my eyes to that. Break my heart for what breaks Yours.

The world doesn't value what You value, God. So help me to live my life in such a way that no one can say anything bad about You. I realize that my time here on earth is short and this life is like a fog. When I'm not spending my time in a way that points my children to You, direct my heart and my actions back into alignment with Your Word and Your ways.

My children see me fail more times than I like to admit. They hear the words I say in anger and see the broken places in my life more than other people do. Give me victory over sin through the power of Your name so that I can be an example to them of what forgiveness looks like. Help me to be humble, Lord, knowing that You work best through my weakness.

Father, I also ask that You would give me opportunities beyond my four walls to use the influence I have for the Kingdom of God. I am Your servant, Your child. Help me to live out the gospel with my life at all times, and if necessary, give me the words to go along with my example.

Praying the Scriptures:

Colossians 3:1-4; 1 Corinthians 10:13; James 1:4; Hebrews 4:15; 2 Corinthians 5:20; 1 John 1:9; James 4:14

Truly, I say to you, unless you turn and become like children, you will never enter the kingdom of heaven.

MATTHEW 18:3, ESV

*N*othing is more endearing than watching a little child learn to walk. Fall down; get up. Fall down. Look for Mom. Get back up. With the slightest encouragement, children will try again. They don't feel the need to explain why they can't walk or make excuses for their failure, because they're aware of their need.

We are born into this world 100 percent dependent on other people. Because of our innate awareness of our need, we start out naturally teachable and humble, which is why Jesus said we should be like children (see Matthew 18:3). As every parent can attest, however, it's not long before our sin nature shows up. Stubbornness and pride kick in the moment we feel that first twinge of self-awareness.

Do you remember that when Satan deceived Adam and Eve, they were immediately aware of their nakedness? Self-awareness is a tricky thing: not enough of it and we can't navigate social situations or advance in our chosen profession or have healthy relationships. Too much self-awareness and we become arrogant and self-centered.

Babies are fun to watch, in part because their self-awareness hasn't kicked in yet. We learn best when we're not hindered by our pride. Pride is a terrible companion on the battlefield. It clouds our judgment, rendering us unable to see our flaws and weaknesses. It robs us of peace and makes us believe that the most important thing is being right.

Jesus said that we should "seek the kingdom of God above all else" (Matthew 6:33). A prideful warrior can't be trusted with the secrets of the Kingdom because pride is self-seeking. We lose sight of the Kingdom when we're too busy looking at ourselves. James 4:6 says, "God opposes the proud but gives grace to the humble." The word James uses for "opposes" is the Greek word *antitasso*, which means "to rage in battle against." So we could also translate James 4:6 this way: "God is in battle against the proud but gives grace to the humble." Imagine God on the battlefield, setting Himself against us. That scenario should strike healthy fear in our hearts! Yet that's what happens when we're full of pride.

Until we humble ourselves, we can't receive the grace God freely offers, and we're lousy at extending it to others. Contrary to what the world says, humility is strength. Humility allows us to be teachable, even as we struggle to learn. Humility says, "I'm sorry. Please forgive me."

It is in our best interest to humble ourselves and become teachable like children. Otherwise we are at war with God and are unable to receive the full blessing of walking in right relationship with Him. Better to humble ourselves than to wait for God to do it.

I'M AT WAR WITH MY FLESH, LORD.

Sometimes the battlefield is my own sinful heart. I confess that I don't like being wrong. I would rather be right—even at the expense of relationships that are dear to me.

In my pride, I don't seek You. That's because my heart doesn't have room for You when pride inhabits it. Quiet my flesh, Father. Don't allow me to think more highly of myself than I should; instead, help me to follow Your example of treating others as more important than myself.

When pride is in my heart, I struggle to show my children Your love. I don't know why I feel the need to have the upper hand when I argue with my kids. It's only when I look back that I hear Your still, small voice and realize I was wrong. I want to love the way You love— with patience and kindness, without envy or boasting or pride.

Help me to be willing to be wrong, especially if it will advance the gospel. Help me to care more about the needs of others so I can see clearly what matters to You. Sometimes pride is like a windshield that needs cleaning: I can't see clearly when pride clouds my view of what really matters.

My children look to me for so many things. They are teachable for such a short time, so while they're teachable, help me to be teachable too. Give me discernment to see beyond my emotions to the root of the issue I'm dealing with. Expose any hint of pride in my life so I can serve You with humility and joy.

You call me to walk in a manner worthy of my calling, with humility, gentleness, and patience. Lord, our world needs humility right now. Our church needs gentleness. Our family needs patience with one another. And I need to be humble before You.

You have told me what is good and what You require of me. Help me to do justice, love kindness, and walk humbly with You. That's what I want for my life. Do whatever it takes to keep those priorities in check. Mold me and shape my heart, even as I'm molding and shaping the hearts of my children.

Let humility rule in our home.

Praying the Scriptures:

PSALM 10:4; 1 CORINTHIANS 13:4; EPHESIANS 4:1-2; MICAH 6:8

A PRAYER *for the* MOM
WHO NEEDS SELF-CONTROL

The fruit of the Spirit is . . . self-control.

GALATIANS 5:22-23, NIV

*I*t's hard to live with eternity in view. With our flesh constantly at war with the Spirit who lives in us, it's easy to see why we say the foolish things we say. Over the course of an ordinary day on the battlefield, we are tempted to lie and to be selfish, rude, impatient, and unkind. Do you see yourself in any of those words? I see myself. Oh, how we all need Jesus!

So how do we keep our lives on the narrow way that Jesus spoke about (see Matthew 7:13)? It might sound easy, but the battle with our flesh is anything but easy.

One approach to dealing with our sinful nature is to make lists of things we shouldn't do. The obvious ones come to mind right away—murder, stealing, adultery. We make mental notes of things that would clearly be in the sin column and skirt around our less caustic shortcomings. Compared to these "big" sins, a lack of self-control might seem insignificant. But without this fruit of the Spirit, we aren't able to experience the full, abundant life God intended for us, and we're prone to eventually slip into more consequential sins.

For instance, we're quick to talk about the sin of pornography, but what would happen if we spent more time asking God to cultivate the fruit of self-control in our lives? The same is true about the consumption of alcohol, a topic that has long been disputed in the church. Christians have differing views on this topic, but I hope we can all agree on one thing: God clearly said that we should not get drunk (see Ephesians 5:18). It's not willpower that keeps us from the sin of drunkenness; it's the fruit of the Spirit called self-control.

Self-control means listening to the gentle prodding of the Holy Spirit and taking it seriously when He says stop! This applies to every area of our lives.

Are you watching a series on Netflix that you'd rather no one else knew about?

Are you procrastinating so you don't have to meet your goal of exercising in the morning?

Are you pushing aside the nudge to be in the Word of God?

Are you struggling with an addiction to sugar or food?

Wherever you're struggling, ask God for self-control, and then listen carefully. He will give you the help you need to have control over your flesh.

Precious mom, our lives speak volumes to our children. When we teach them that the Christian life is all about a list of dos and don'ts, we can easily miss the heart of walking in right relationship with God.

I ADMIT IT, LORD. I struggle to be self-controlled.

So here I am again, on my knees, humbled by my need for You. You are my only true source of strength. The truth is, I need You every minute of the day! I realize that apart from Your intervention, I won't have the victory I so desperately want. It's not by might or by power but by Your Spirit that I can see the fruit of self-control in my life.

Lord, I'm leaning hard into Your grace today. Your grace has brought me salvation, and now it trains me to say no to what would hold me back from You. Your grace allows me to live a self-controlled, upright, godly life. It's not easy to live this way in the world today, Lord. I know I'm not alone in this. Many of your children are struggling to live a set-apart life right now, including me.

Help me to model self-control to my children. The next time I want to yell at my child or say that thing I thought I'd never even think, remind me that Your Spirit will enable me to choose the high road.

As I walk out this life, I'm trying to hear Your voice. Help me not to mistake the "good" voice that encourages legalistic behavior for

Your voice. I know that legalism robs me of the joy of listening to Your voice every moment, so please fill me with Your Spirit instead.

I want my children to see You at work in me, even in my broken places. Let them see humility and a desire to be set free from my flesh. Help me to discipline my body and keep it under control so that I can run the race You have set before me and finish well.

Lord, this parenting thing is hard! It's so much harder—and so much richer—than I ever dreamed. Open my eyes so I can see the heart issues in my children. Rather than impose a harsh sentence based on rules, show me the best way to teach them Your heart. I want to love my children the way You love them.

Thank You, Lord, that through You, all things are possible! I praise You for what You have done and for what You are doing.

Praying the Scriptures:

Colossians 1:29; Zechariah 4:6; Titus 2:11-12;
1 Corinthians 9:27; Philippians 4:13; Mark 10:27

FOR *the* WEARY WARRIOR

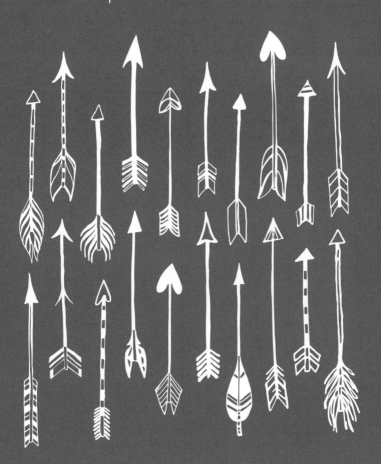

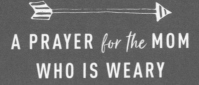

A PRAYER *for the* MOM
WHO IS WEARY

Come to me, all of you who are weary and carry
heavy burdens, and I will give you rest.

MATTHEW 11:28

*A*re you weary? It's no wonder. Moms today are busier
than ever. We're signing our kids up for everything from
athletics to music and the arts. Most moms I know are
exhausted, worn-out women who admit to feeling
guilty if they don't provide their children with every
imaginable opportunity. These moms are running from
sunup to sundown, often sacrificing their own margin
and time with the Lord, and they're left feeling weary
and disillusioned. We're running ragged. Just. So. Busy.

I wonder: Is there a spiritual component to this
busyness? If everything we do carries eternal significance, then surely our Creator must have something to
say about our everyday decisions. Even when we sign
up for soccer.

We are doing holy work, you know.

Families are pressed on every side on this battlefield of busyness. And it *is* a battlefield. Tired parents are a favorite target of the devil, because tired parents are prone to compromise. Tired parents tune out and tend to miss subtle signals from struggling teens. Tired moms are more likely to compromise with a tantruming toddler, choosing comfort over correction. (Ask me how I know.)

I'm not talking about unavoidable seasons of stress here. Every mother has seasons that defy rest. There are seasons of newborns, moving, and career transitions, just to name a few. But when your calendar is so full you can barely breathe and you know in your heart you're too tired to properly train your children, it's time to pause and assess your priorities. Does your lifestyle allow you to pursue God with your children?

The Bible is full of stories about men and women like you and me who made decisions on their own without coming before the Lord. The results of those decisions range from disappointing to disastrous. I know, I know, I'm talking about things like soccer practice and youth theater. But if it seems inconsequential to sign up for something without prayer, consider this: one of the primary weapons of the enemy is distraction. I can think of many times when my casual yes resulted in months of compromise-driven parenting and a weakened sense of spiritual discernment.

Before you allow the opportunities of mothering to distract you from the mission of motherhood, look to the Lord. Look to the future. It's not so far away. The time we've been given to influence our children is short, and the temptation to overfill our calendars is real.

If the Spirit is speaking to you about this, know that a change in this area won't be without conflict. If you're in the habit of proceeding without praying, this habit will be a weapon the devil will try to use against you. He will actively oppose any attempts you make to live the way God would have you live. Don't listen to him. Persevere, beloved mother of future warriors! God's rest is always found in obedience. Don't look at what anyone else is doing—look to God, and He will direct your path.

Do you have a decision to make right now? Pray first, then prioritize, making sure your plans line up with God's. After that, proceed with confidence. God is with you!

I'M TIRED, LORD.

I can't remember when I last spoke to You about the little decisions that make up my everyday life. They feel unimportant when I'm making them, but I'm starting to see that all those little decisions I make without You leave me feeling tired and worn out.

I confess that it's easy for me to compromise in my parenting. My spiritual eyes can grow dim amid a never-ending stream of demands on my time and energy. I have little time left for You—and it shows.

You are the Prince of Peace, and I need Your peace more than ever. I need Your Spirit to control my mind so I can have life and peace according to Your Word. Will You remind me that the peace I seek is never found apart from Your grace?

You say that I can come to You and find rest for my soul. I hear Your gentle voice saying, "Come to Me, all of you who are weary, and I will give you rest." I need the kind of rest that You offer, Lord. So today I come before You and ask for Your rest.

My family is busy—maybe too busy. Lord, would You direct us as we make decisions about where to invest our time and energy? Would You give us peace as a family? Help us to wisely prioritize the things we say yes to. I know You have a plan for us, Father, and I know it's a good one. You have a plan to prosper our family and not to harm us; You have a plan to give us a hope and a future.

Give us rest as a family. Quiet my heart so I can hear from You more clearly. Open my eyes to anything that distracts my family and me from accomplishing all that You have created us to do.

Help me to fix my eyes on You, not on what another family has or does. I need You to keep my mind in perfect peace as I focus on Your will for my life. Give me the courage to say no to the things that are not part of Your plan and to say yes to the things You're directing me to do.

I'm going to do my best to pray about everything, telling You what

I need and thanking You for all You have done. I know that when I do this, I'll experience Your peace, which exceeds anything I can understand.

Praying the Scriptures:

Isaiah 9:6; Romans 8:6; Matthew 11:28-30; Jeremiah 29:11; Isaiah 26:3-4; Philippians 4:6-7

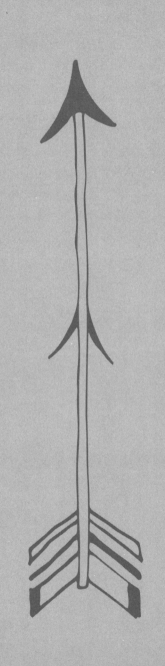

A PRAYER *for the* MOM
WHO'S FACING *the* UNEXPECTED

What can I say? He has spoken to me, and he himself
has done this. I will walk humbly all my years because
of this anguish of my soul.

ISAIAH 38:15, NIV

Like anyone else alive and old enough to remember that
day, I will never forget where I was when the planes hit
the World Trade Center in New York. Even though Jay
and I were watching from thousands of miles away from
our home in northern Washington State, our hearts
were breaking in unison with millions of others as we
watched the tragedy unfold on live television.

In the months that followed, our nation desperately
tried to make sense of what can't be reasoned away.
Unspeakable suffering came over our country. That day
served as a sobering reminder that there are questions
in this world we'll never have answers to this side of
heaven.

As a resident of planet Earth, I am assured of this: there will be suffering. There will be unexpected sorrow. Terrorism is an all-too-frequent occurrence in our world today, brought on as a result of wickedness in the human heart. But how do we respond when the source of suffering is less obvious? What do you do when your child is diagnosed with a devastating illness or a loved one is injured in an accident? These are hard questions. But God hasn't left us alone on the battlefield of human suffering.

We don't know what trials lie ahead for us, but God assures us that He will be with us no matter what comes. God uses suffering and trials to develop patience in us. The psalmist David writes that he was thankful for his sufferings because they taught him to keep God's commands (see Psalm 119:71). We may not understand why God allows suffering, but we can be assured of three things: (1) God will use our suffering for His glory and our sanctification (see 1 Peter 1:6-7); (2) God's heart toward us is always, ever, only good (see Romans 8:28); and (3) we will be blessed if we persevere under trials (see James 1:12).

So how do we respond when we're blindsided on the battlefield? We pray.

Prayer is like air in the lungs of the one who trusts the Lord. It's the way we live—and the way we stand when the burdens of this life seem unbearable. James said, "Are any of you suffering hardships? You should pray" (James 5:13). The question is rhetorical, of course, since we will all face suffering at some point. James is reminding us that prayer should be our first response, not our last resort.

There is nothing God can't accomplish. And this all-powerful God invites us to come to Him in prayer—about everything.

If you are struggling with an unexpected trial—if you're the victim of abuse, if a friend has abandoned you, if your child is suffering, if you're the victim of gossip, if you're being criticized or taken advantage of—your first response should be to pray.

This is Battlefield 101—knowing that we can take our requests to God and He will answer us and help us. As children of God and as mothers, prayer must be our passion.

No matter the circumstance—and no matter how unexpected it is—the answer is prayer.

I DIDN'T SEE THIS COMING, LORD.

I wasn't ready. My heart is broken, my eyes are burning from the salt of my tears. My body hurts—a reminder that this world is not my home. I am crying out to You, Lord. I'm struggling to understand.

Words don't come easily on this battlefield, God, but I want to praise You here. I know that there is power in praising You, so I lift trembling hands and praise You. Here in this place, with my human condition so apparent, I put my trust in You. You are so far beyond me—it's impossible for me to understand Your decisions and Your ways. But I do know this: everything exists by Your power. It's all here for Your glory.

I want to give You glory in this place, God. I want to give You glory in my brokenness. You promise that the one who remains steadfast under trials will receive the crown of life, which You have promised to those who love You. I love You, Lord, and I long to love You more.

I'm clinging to Your promises right now. I'm holding fast to the knowledge that You are good. I believe that my sufferings are nothing compared to the glory that You will reveal later. Help me to stand in the knowledge that You are working all things, even the hard things, together for my good.

I know that good things are coming, Lord, because *You* are coming. You are my deliverer! When I think back on my life and remember Your faithfulness, I am overwhelmed. I put my hope in You, knowing that You will continue to deliver me and my children through the prayers of Your people.

Thank You for the way You graciously answer prayer. I trust You, no matter the outcome of the situation I'm facing. I trust that You are working behind the scenes in ways I can't comprehend, for an outcome that will be for my good.

Help me to communicate trust to my children. I want them to see that You are good, so help me, even in my brokenness, to display a faith that says "I trust You." Keep my heart close to You, Lord. Draw me to You through prayer. Lead me to friendships with others who will pray with me, and let me be encouraged through the prayers of Your people.

Your Word says that the prayers of a righteous person are powerful and effective, so help me to be that righteous person, that woman of prayer.

Praying the Scriptures:

1 PETER 1:6-7; JAMES 1:1-18; ROMANS 11:33-36; JAMES 1:12; ROMANS 8:18; PSALM 18:2; 2 CORINTHIANS 1:10-11; JAMES 5:16

DARE *to* HOPE

A PRAYER *for the* PARENT *of a* PRODIGAL

> On my bed I remember you, I think of you
> through the watches of the night.
>
> PSALM 63:6, NIV

I didn't understand why there's a flower called baby's breath until I had my first child. There is something so sweet and pure about those first few weeks of newborn life, right down to the air they exhale. When my children were small, I loved to breathe it in, and I could get absolutely lost in their tiniest movements and sounds.

I recall the wonder I felt the first time I held each of my seven precious babies. Joy comes after hours of labor, and that first beautiful cry fills the room.

Our children are a wonder, aren't they? Beautiful fingers, tiny toes—we want to take it all in, not missing a moment. Nothing can rival the bond between a mother and her child. When our children are born to us, our dreams for them are born too. A mother imagines milestones and birthdays and Christmases that have never been with a life she has only just met. The future is bright.

But the future can't be predicted by human hearts, and life rarely follows the path we prescribe for it. Children born into this broken world are often tempted away from the One who made them, and when they stray, it hurts.

We can't choose for our precious children—they must choose for themselves. And there's nothing quite like the anguish a prodigal child can inflict on his or her parents. The sorrow is real—and no one understands this more than the heavenly Father. God knows what it's like to look with wonder at His special creation, to revel in each beautiful feature, to have plans and hopes and dreams—and to long for His children to come home.

God understands the pain of rejection and the consequences of sin. In fact, He gave His own Son as a ransom for our children—a love so severe that God turned His back on His own Son in order to save us and our children.

Precious mom, if your heart is breaking right now, know that God's heart breaks too. This battlefield, the battlefield of the prodigal child, is a lonely place, but long after you have cried the last tear over your child tonight and turned out your light, God will still be awake.

Let's lock arms in prayer together and declare what

we know to be true: the battle we're fighting isn't ours. It is God's. So keep praying. Keep trusting. Keep communicating.

Most of all, keep hoping. Hope is more than wishing that things will work out the way we want them to. It's resting in the arms of the almighty, all-knowing God. It's trusting that He sees everything and is always at work.

Let God work the night shift.

LORD, MY CHILD HAS wandered far from You.

I never realized how much Your Father heart must ache for Your lost children . . . until now. I never understood how fierce the spiritual battle is . . . until now. And I've never wanted anything more than to see my lost sheep come home.

This hurt is deep, God. You said that I would have trouble in this world, and sure enough, I'm in trouble. It's easy for me to wonder what I might have done to prevent this from happening. I can hear the devil whisper his lies, saying I'm a failure and that this is my fault. If I'm honest, I know I haven't always been the parent You want me to be. But You also say that You have overcome the world.

Help me to listen to Your voice alone as I walk this long, hard road. Turn my eyes to Your Word. Tune my ears to Your voice, even as I struggle to be free from the voice of my accuser.

Lord, my mother's heart is broken. You know the pain of having a wayward child. I take comfort in knowing that You understand exactly what I'm going through. Your Word in Psalm 56:8 says that You keep track of all my sorrows and You keep a record of my tears. Thank You that You understand my sorrow.

I see the spiritual battle more clearly than ever, Lord. Thank You that You will fight those who fight You and You will save Your children. Please break the bondage of sin that has captured my precious child. Bring people to direct my lost lamb back to You.

Give me wisdom as I shepherd my prodigal. Don't let my heart become cold out of self-protection or frustration. Instead, help me to love this child deeply, because love covers a multitude of sins. Help me to avoid strife and recognize the foolishness of being quick to argue. Instead, help me to be slow to anger, knowing that my temper will only lead to harm.

I know that nothing is too hard for You. You are good to those who hope in You, to those who seek You. You say it's good to wait quietly for Your salvation, so please give me the grace I need to wait for You. While I wait, I praise You. This child is Yours, so now I give my child back to You. Right now I dare to hope because You are good. You are my hope—and You are the hope of my child.

Please bring my child back home, Lord.

Praying the Scriptures:

JOHN 16:33; ISAIAH 1:2; ISAIAH 49:25; 1 PETER 4:8; PROVERBS 20:3; PSALM 37:8; LUKE 15; JEREMIAH 32:27; LAMENTATIONS 3:25-26

A PRAYER *for the* WORRIED MOM

Don't worry about anything; instead, pray about everything. Tell God what you need, and thank him for all he has done.

PHILIPPIANS 4:6

"*W*orry is God-forgetting." That's what a dear friend said when I finally decided to tell her about my private struggle with worry. My confession came after years of silent desperation, after I realized I was on the losing end of my lifelong battle with anxiety. I was disappointed in myself. Without even realizing it, I was finding my identity in a few human-made titles that helped me push my silent struggle to the back burner. Rather than admitting I was a woman who struggled with anxiety, I clung to my identity as a Bible teacher, a pastor's wife, a homeschooling mom. From the outside, my life looked picture perfect. But on the inside, it was anything but.

I have struggled my whole life with anxiety. In my twenties and thirties, it was often over the top—a reminder of the childhood abuse and heartache I'd faced. Anxiety in and of itself isn't sin. For me, it has been a reminder of how dependent I am on the Lord. But there comes a point when anxiety crosses over into something God calls sin. At this point in my life, I realized that my worry had become a stumbling block on the battlefield of my life.

I say this with a fair amount of trepidation because I know the pain that chronic anxiety brings. I believe there's a time to be tender with people who are struggling with worry and a time when we need a strong call to action. For me, it was obvious that I needed a wake-up call. A troubling thought would make its way into my mind, and I would camp on it until it became the only thing I could think about. That's what I was doing when my friend reminded me that I had taken God out of the equation of my worry.

What she was lovingly saying was "Heidi, you're sinning." It was an "ouch" moment—but in the best possible way. By God's grace, her gentle reminder hit its intended target and the defenses of my flesh stood down. As a result, my heart was turned upward instead of inward.

As mothers, we have many opportunities to worry. We lose sleep over medical mysteries, financial frustrations, wandering hearts, and wayward children—just to name a few. But Jesus instructs us to not worry about tomorrow. The Bible plainly says we're not to worry about even the most basic things: food and clothing.

God knows we're made of dust, beloved. He knows what our hearts can take. He's aware of the land mines that are buried deep on the battlefield of anxiety and worry, and He says, "Don't worry. I've got you."

Are you worried, precious mom? Turn your eyes upon Jesus. Quiet your heart and mind, and as you do, cast your cares on the One who can take every single burden and replace it with peace.

FATHER, I'M STRUGGLING WITH WORRY.

I know You say not to worry, but I can't seem to help it. Sorrow is everywhere in this world. Terrorism is in my own backyard. Political lines have created tension in my community and even in my church. Lies have permeated the culture. And there are things to worry about closer to home too, like bullies and frenemies (oh, Lord, You know I've had a few of those). I confess that worry makes me feel like at least I'm doing *something*, but in reality, I'm draining myself of the strength that comes from placing my cares at Your feet.

Father, help me to not be anxious about my life, my body, what I'll eat or drink, or even what I should wear. I want to believe that life is more than food and my body is more than clothing, but my flesh stands in staunch opposition to Your Spirit.

The next time I'm tempted to worry about whether our next paycheck will cover that unexpected medical bill or the higher rent, help me to look at the birds of the air. Help me notice how they don't reap or gather into barns, because they know You will feed them. These precious creatures are a reminder to me that though You love all You have made, my children and I are even more valuable than they are.

I know I need to take life one day at a time, Lord. But sometimes all the days seem to pile on at once, and I wonder whether Your grace will be enough. Help me to not borrow trouble by worrying about tomorrow, for tomorrow will have enough worries of its own. Jesus, You showed us how to do life best. Help me to not worry about anything, but instead to pray about everything. God, You know my needs already, so I thank You for all You have already done. I want to experience Your peace, which exceeds anything I can understand. I ask that Your peace would guard my heart and my mind in Christ Jesus.

I pray that my children would see a mom who is more warrior than worrier, Lord. Help me to guard my heart against the sin of pride, which keeps me from humbling myself before You. I know You care for me and for my family. Help me to cast all my cares on You in full confidence that You are able to carry them.

Your Word says that a tranquil heart is life to the body. I ask for that life today, Lord. Please give me the grace to seek tranquility instead of trouble.

Praying the Scriptures:

Matthew 6:24-34; Philippians 4:6-7; Matthew 6:8;
1 Peter 5:6-7; Proverbs 14:30

A PRAYER *for the* BROKENHEARTED MOM

You will experience God's peace, which exceeds anything we can understand. His peace will guard your hearts and minds as you live in Christ Jesus.

PHILIPPIANS 4:7

On June 27, 2017, my family got a phone call that changed our lives forever.

At approximately 11:30 p.m., my sister called to tell me that her son had been in a car accident. In the hours that followed, we heard words that no one wants to hear: my nephew's neck was broken, rendering him a quadriplegic. His brain had suffered a devastating injury known as DAI, or diffuse axonal injury, which—translated into something we could understand—was the adult version of shaken baby syndrome.

The impact of the accident had left Bobby with a crushed skull and a broken neck. The artery that supplied blood to his brain had been severed in the crash.

Paramedics didn't think he would survive the ambulance ride to the trauma center in Portland, Oregon, where we were waiting. The prognosis looked grim.

This battlefield was unknown to us. The landscape offered little hope, and it seemed that every possible outcome was devastating. We were heartbroken—but we were not alone.

God's mercy took on new meaning for me that night. You see, this particular kind of sorrow requires a particular kind of mercy, one that I'd never asked for before. I'd reserved it for other people.

Until that night, I had wondered how people breathe when they are given devastating news. Now I know. God's peace, which truly does surpass understanding (see Philippians 4:7) met us in those weeks and months. Because of God's grace, we were able to walk through a devastating diagnosis with peace.

Our weeks at the hospital were filled with agonizing, praying, and waiting. Then one day Bobby woke up from his coma—much to the surprise of his doctors. He is still working to regain the use of his arms and legs. We talk about Bobby's story of healing all the time around here, but to me, the miracle of God's peace was just as amazing as the miracle of his physical survival.

As Christians, we don't grieve the way the world does. Because of Jesus, we grieve with hope (see 1 Thessalonians 4:13). Because of Jesus, we can trust in the goodness of God. If God was willing to sacrifice His own beloved Son, He can be trusted with anything we're facing too. Even the big thing you're facing right now.

I'M NOT READY FOR THIS BATTLE, LORD.

Are You here? Are You in my valley with me? Are You here in the valley of the shadow of death? My dreams are shattered in this valley, Father. I wonder if I can go on.

Father, I hurt. Every part of my being is in pain. I am no match for this giant. I don't know the broken terrain of this battlefield. I didn't train to fight on this battlefield. I've only heard other people talk about it, and it seems like they know You better than I do.

My mind tells me that You're good; I know the verses by heart. But somehow, in this place, I need to hear directly from You. Would You allow heaven to touch earth in such a way that I know it's You? I need to feel Your touch, hear Your voice, be reminded of Your love. Remind me that You are always, only, ever good.

I've heard You called Jehovah Rapha, our healer. Would you heal even this? I've heard of Your healing, but only in the lives of other people. Somehow I am now that "other person." Now it's my people who are hurting. It's my sorrow. My valley.

The hopelessness that threatens to undo me is real, and we both know it. Even so, I know that You love me and Your will is best, so even as I struggle for the words, help me to pray for Your will. You invite me to ask You for what I want, so I come before You honestly, asking for a miracle. But I also submit my will to Yours, trusting You to do the kind of miracle You know is best.

Help me to not give up too soon. I'm waiting. Lord, I believe in You, but I'm weary. Give me the strength and grace I need to face each decision, each day—sometimes each minute.

Have mercy, Lord. Not only do I need to recognize Your goodness in this for myself, but I also want to be able to tell others of Your goodness. When others doubt Your heart in this situation, will You give me the words to describe this thing that has no words?

I used to think that pain like this was unsurvivable. And yet here I am. I wasn't sure I could breathe under this kind of sorrow, but somehow my heart keeps beating in rhythm with my tears.

I can't see the way right now—all I have is You. You are the God of hope, and I need something to hang on to. So I'm hanging on to You, broken heart and all.

Praying the Scriptures:

Psalm 23; Romans 5:3; James 1:2-4, 12; Romans 8:18

Section 6

BEYOND *the* BATTLEFIELD

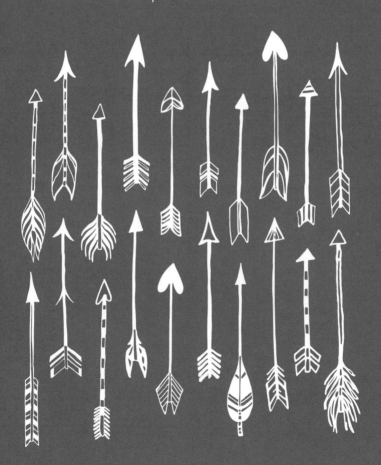

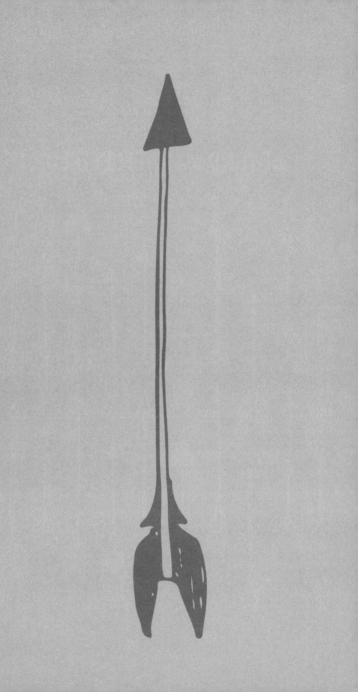

These words that I command you today shall be on your heart. You shall teach them diligently to your children.

DEUTERONOMY 6:6, ESV

*O*ne of the saddest passages in the Bible is Judges 2:10-12. Check it out:

After that generation died, another generation grew up who did not acknowledge the LORD or remember the mighty things he had done for Israel.

The Israelites did evil in the LORD's sight and served the images of Baal. They abandoned the LORD, the God of their ancestors, who had brought them out of Egypt. They went after other gods, worshiping the gods of the people around them. And they angered the LORD.

After Joshua and the entire first generation who entered the Promised Land died, the next generation served false gods. Like me, maybe you're thinking, *Hey, wait a minute! God gave them the Promised Land. God answered their prayers. What happened?*

Lean in, beloved, because this is important. Verse 10 explains how this could have happened. The parents of this generation—people who had been through so much, who had seen God's power, and who knew of His goodness—failed in their most important job. They didn't teach their children about the Lord or tell them about the work He had done for Israel. The result of their failure to teach their children to love and serve God resulted in unimaginable suffering for generations to come.

There is a war going on for the hearts and minds of an entire generation. Much is at stake. Our adversary isn't going to sit the next one out. He's waiting like a stealthy lion for a generation to stop declaring the faithfulness of God to their children. As we see in the book of Judges, the disobedience of just one generation can set the next generation up for failure.

We're not so unlike the Israelites of old, are we? Look around the Christian community today. How are we doing at shepherding God's children? Are we holding fast to the authority and unchanging truth contained in God's Word? Are we making sure to tell the next generation about God's faithfulness?

You see, it takes only one generation to lose the spiritual legacy that needs to be passed on. After we're gone from this earth, what will our legacy be? Our children are looking to us to shepherd them on the battlefield. If we fail to instruct them in the ways of God, we are opening the door for the enemy to set up camp in our hearts and homes. Let's not give him the opportunity.

We are called to train up our children in the ways of the Lord, to do everything we can to offer them a cool drink of living water from God's Word. We're called to take up our weapons daily, starting with prayer. So pray for your children, precious mom. Pray for them by name. Tell them the story of God's unending faithfulness, and then entrust them to the Lord.

While God doesn't promise that our children will choose to follow Him, He does promise that there is a blessing in obedience. Like the Israelites, we're not responsible for the outcome, but we are responsible to walk in obedience.

The results are up to God.

I WANT MY CHILDREN TO WALK WITH YOU, LORD.

I know these precious children of mine are gifts from You. They are blessings, arrows in Your hand. Thank You for entrusting them to me.

Honestly, there are days when I just don't care if I train them or not. Sometimes the sheer demands of parenting get the best of me, and I don't pick up my Bible for days or weeks or even months. I neglect to set aside time to teach my children about You, leaving that responsibility up to my pastor or to Sunday school teachers. I see now that this is sin. Please forgive me for not recognizing who is behind the temptation to put You last. I know that the enemy has his eye on the target—the next generation.

Like the Israelites, I often forget about the blessings You've given me in the past. When my life is easy, I all too quickly forget about You. Lord, I don't want to forget! Please help me to be consistent and joyful in remembering You in my own life and in instructing my children in Your ways. I want to teach Your commands diligently to my children, to talk about them when we sit at home and when we walk along the road, when we go to bed and when we wake up.

I recognize that I'm responsible for teaching my children about You—not my pastor, not their teachers. Me. Father, give me a pressing desire to see my children walk with You. I lift them to You by name right now:

Lord, help me to set a godly example for my family. Help me to love You with all my heart, all my soul, all my mind, and all my strength. Help me to keep Your commands always before me. I pray for this generation of parents as we face lies on the battlefield of the human heart like never before. Make us bold so that we can see the truth and then speak that truth in love, passing it on to our children. Thank You that You will never leave us or forsake us as we do this important work.

Praying the Scriptures:

PSALM 127:3-4; DEUTERONOMY 6:4-7; EPHESIANS 4:15;
PROVERBS 22:6; EPHESIANS 6:4; HEBREWS 13:5

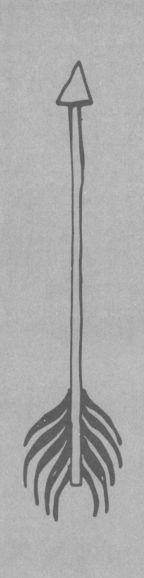

THE SHEEP *of* HIS PASTURE

A PRAYER *for the* MOM WHO
WANTS *to* SHEPHERD *like* JESUS

The LORD is my shepherd; I have all that I need.

PSALM 23:1

*T*here is no doubt that being a warrior is a big part of mothering, but that is only half of the story. Consider this: one side of you must be all warrior—suited up, ready for battle, prepared for every scenario. An archer-in-training. The other side must be tender and protective. That sounds a lot like our Father, doesn't it? In Psalm 23, perhaps the most familiar and best-loved psalm in Scripture, we get a glimpse into the softer side of God's Father heart.

In this psalm, we see David's struggles: he's weary from battle, fearing injury and enemies and even death. David's struggles are familiar to us, aren't they? Psalm 23 offers a beautiful picture of the Father's gentle, fierce love for His children, and it resonates with all of us— parents of prodigals, the mother who has suffered the pain of divorce and rejection, the mother who has stood over her child's fresh grave.

From the first cries of newborn life to the final labored breath of a weary warrior, Psalm 23 reminds us that God is always with us. It also reminds us that we are called to shepherd our own children in much the same way that God shepherds us. We can't read this psalm without noticing that it is written from the perspective of a sheep. Just as we are God's sheep, our children are ours. We are our children's first introduction to the Good Shepherd.

As you read Psalm 23, see yourself as a shepherd to your own children.

The LORD is my shepherd; I have all that I need.

Notice that our Shepherd doesn't mention our wants. Instead, He sees that we have all we need.

He lets me rest in green meadows; he leads me beside peaceful streams. He renews my strength.

Our Good Shepherd provides an oasis for His sheep. In times of stress, am I a place of peace and rest for my children?

He guides me along right paths, bringing honor
to his name.

Am I leading my children along right paths? Our
children are following our lead; they are watching our
every move.

Even when I walk through the darkest valley,
I will not be afraid, for you are close beside me.

A spirit of fear has no place in the life of a believer.
Does my child see me reacting in fear or in faith?

Your rod and your staff protect and comfort me.

A good shepherd knows that discipline is protection.
God disciplines those He loves.

You prepare a feast for me in the presence of my
enemies.

This is Papa Bear coming through loud and clear!
You gonna mess with my beloved? Watch while I prepare a feast for them in front of you!

You honor me by anointing my head with oil.
My cup overflows with blessings.

This is a reminder to praise my children. When they leave home, I want them to know that they are treasured and loved.

Surely your goodness and unfailing love will pursue me all the days of my life, and I will live in the house of the LORD forever.

God's heart is to pursue His own. As a mother, I want to offer unconditional love to my children too.

What a good Shepherd we have!

FATHER, THANK YOU FOR the way You gently shepherd Your children.

Thank You for the overwhelming provision You give us. My soul is reminded of Your goodness—it is refreshing to this weary sheep's parched tongue.

Thank You for so beautifully meeting all my needs and the needs of my family. As I look over my life, Your fingerprints are everywhere. Evidence of Your love surrounds me. Father, would You help me to shepherd my children the way You shepherd me?

My Shepherd, You are able to accomplish infinitely more than I could ask or think. Your provision is always more than enough. It is abundant!

I know that my family and I may walk through some dark valleys in the days to come. Would You teach me how to walk through tough times in a way that brings honor and glory to You? Would You help me to shepherd my children through valleys of fear and temptation? Would You invade our home with Your Spirit as I teach my children to stay on Your path?

Father, I don't always like to discipline my children. Sometimes it's a matter of being too tired or too busy—too distracted by other things that feel more pressing. Yet I take comfort in the strength of Your kind discipline in my own life. Help me to discipline my children in such a way that they are drawn closer to You. Help me to use my staff to pry my sheep loose from brambles, pushing path-altering branches aside in order to keep them on Your path.

My shepherd's heart is fearful at times, Lord. This world we're walking through has some dangerous paths, filled with dark, unfamiliar turns. Keep me close to You, my Good Shepherd, and help me to keep my sheep close too. Even though we may walk through the valley of the shadow of death, help us not to fear but to keep our eyes always on You.

Thank You that we have heaven to look forward to and that until we arrive home, Your goodness and mercy will follow us all the days of our lives. As I teach my children to trust You, please keep this eternal destination always before me. Thank You that You never stop loving, never stop pursuing, and never stop protecting Your own.

You are the Good Shepherd!

Praying the Scriptures:

PSALM 23; EPHESIANS 3:20

THE SNARE *of* OFFENSE

A PRAYER *for the* MOM
STRUGGLING *with* BITTERNESS

Get rid of all bitterness.

EPHESIANS 4:31, NIV

I was stewing. All day.

Never mind—I'd been stewing for a week. You know . . . like a good batch of homemade bone broth. Every thought about the situation, every bit of mistrust about this person I'd ever had had been leached out of me as I stewed.

Now, I love a bowl of good, hearty bone broth. The whole reason bone broth is so good for you is that all the vitamins and minerals are cooked out of the bones in a slow-cooking process that takes hours and hours. But there's a point in the stewing process when the heat goes from making the broth amazing to ruining it.

I had reached that "overdone" point with my friend. She had hurt me. Maybe it was intentional, maybe it wasn't—but it was eating me alive. So I sat there working on a ministry project, stewing in a steaming bowl of self-pity. Isn't that classic? I can see the headlines for the devil's newspaper now: "Bible Teacher Caught in Snare of Offense." I was allowing the enemy to seduce me with clever-sounding arguments. See if you recognize any of them:

- *I don't deserve this.*
- *I thought she was my friend.*
- *This was supposed to turn out differently.*
- *I feel used and betrayed.*
- *My anger is justified.*

And just like that, I was sidelined—taken off the battlefield because I was allowing the accuser of my soul to use my own pain against me. My hunch is that you can relate. The Greek word for "offense" is *skandalon*, which is the part of a trap where bait is hung. We are so easily caught up in this snare of offense, but fortunately God has made a way out. Are you ready for it?

It's prayer.

If you're struggling with a hurt that you can't let go of, or if you notice that you're easily offended, try these steps:

Confess your offended state as sin. The apostle Paul says, "Get rid of all bitterness, rage, anger, harsh words, and slander, as well as all types of evil behavior" (Ephesians 4:31). Notice that Paul doesn't make any allowances for why you might be bitter. This doesn't excuse any sin the other person may have committed against you, but God knows that bitterness can take a warrior out of the fight.

Refuse to let bitterness take root. Hebrews 12:15 says, "Look after each other so that none of you fails to receive the grace of God. Watch out that no poisonous root of bitterness grows up to trouble you, corrupting many." The next time you allow a little root of bitterness to settle in an unseen place in your heart, picture a tree root that has ruined a sidewalk by pushing its way through the concrete. Roots are powerful, and they can end up taking us down.

Pray for the person who hurt you. Really pray. This doesn't mean the person is off the hook or even that you have to renew a relationship with him or her; it just means you're letting God handle that person. You'll know you've released the person who hurt you when you can pray for God's blessing in his or her life without crying. And if you're still in the crying phase of forgiving, that's okay. God understands.

Beloved, there is a blessing in extending forgiveness. Untangle your heart from any hint of bitterness. After all, you've got Kingdom work to do! Don't let the enemy sideline you through the snare of offense. Remember—you can't give your kids what you don't have! Let go. Live free.

I'M JUST SO HURT, LORD.

Honestly, it feels good to mull it over, thinking of all the ways I was wronged. Somehow I think it will dull the pain, but instead I just feel worse. I need Your help to stop feeling sorry for myself. I confess my self-pity as sin and ask You to forgive me for staying in a state of offense.

Father, my kids are watching me as I struggle through feelings of betrayal and sadness. A friendship that held so much potential for the Kingdom was lost in a single moment, and I can't make sense of it. Will You help me to show my children how to walk this out in a way that brings You glory? Something tells me I'm going to have to die to myself—over and over—in order to do this.

As I pray now, I'm reminded of the times I've inflicted pain on other people myself. Please make my heart tender toward the person who caused me pain. Help me to forgive others in the same way You forgive me: without holding back.

Lord, help me to show my children what it looks like to be kind and compassionate to others, forgiving just as He forgave me in Christ. I know that my children will face rejection at some point themselves, and I want to set an example for them. I need Your wisdom to guide them through their own rough places.

Please bless the person who hurt me in every area of their life. Every time I feel the sting of past offenses bubbling to the surface of my heart, prompt me to pray. Guard my heart, and give me victory over the snare of offense. Give me the grace to remember who I am in You.

As Your beloved child, help me to put on compassion, kindness, humility, meekness, and patience. Help me to be quick to forgive and quick to seek forgiveness because I know that You have forgiven me. Above all, Jesus, please help me to put on love because I know love binds everything together in perfect harmony.

Praying the Scriptures:

1 Kings 19:4-5; Proverbs 15:13; Psalm 73; Colossians 3:12-14

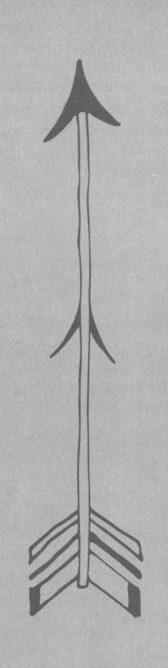

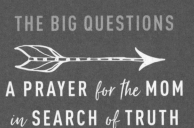
Listen, for I will speak of excellent things, and from the opening of my lips will come right things; for my mouth will speak truth.

PROVERBS 8:6, NKJV

How do we define truth? Is there even such a thing?

Those are questions the "Google generation" is struggling to answer—even though Alexa can start our coffee makers and make sure our Crock-Pot gets turned to low as we race home in rush hour. And speaking of traffic . . . concerned about the traffic from Seattle to Portland? No problem—just ask your phone. Wondering about the forecast in Lee's Summit, Missouri? No problem—Google knows.

Still, answers to the larger questions of life elude us.

Where do we come from? Where are we going? Is God real? Does He care? Are the wages of our sin *really* death? These are the same questions people have been asking since before we were born onto this battlefield. It's the same battle with the enemy of our soul—just different tactics. Have you seen a change in tactic from your own childhood to now? Me, too.

Remember: every demon at Satan's command is on a mission to deceive God's people. How the evil one goes about this—his battle plan, strategies, and tactics—changes from one generation to the next. Today our children are caught in the crosshairs of a cultural and spiritual crisis. Everywhere we look, we face blatant denials of God's created order—all of which are boldly marketed to our children through media, education, and movies.

Human beings, arrogant as we are, have always sought to take credit away from God, and this is just the latest attempt. New generation = new tactic. Precious mom, I wish I could hold your hand tightly right now and remind you of this unchanging truth: worldly wisdom will never match the wisdom of the Creator.

The next time your children ask you a question you're unsure how to answer, turn to the Word. Though the world is changing daily, God assures us that He doesn't change. From alcohol to abortion, gender to genetics, parenting to marriage, and even the origin of the universe itself, God is still speaking His unchanging truth through His Word.

One caveat that we must not miss: our words will

hurt instead of heal if they aren't bathed in love. It's not enough to know the Word; we must apply it with gentleness and love. You can be confident in God's ability to help you see—and speak—truth. Though lies are all around us, God's truth will prevail. But along the way, we can't forget that the greatest of these is love. First and always, we are called to love.

The truth. In love. Any other way is not God's way.

HELP ME TO LOVE PEOPLE LIKE YOU DO, LORD.

My children have been born in a confusing time—and I'm often just as confused as they are. Lord, I need You now more than ever. My instinct is to run from topics that confuse or embarrass me, but You have asked me to be Your ambassador in a world that is lost. Would You help me to speak the truth in love? Would you help me to grow more and more like Christ? I want to be an example of truth and love. Let no abusive talk come out of my mouth, but only what is good and helpful for encouraging those who are listening.

I want to speak the truth with boldness and gentleness. You have saved me, Lord! You have given me hope, and because of this hope, I can be bold. Help me to set an example of warrior-like wisdom on this battlefield of deception. But also give me a gentle tongue. Help me to avoid speaking harshly to my children when I see things in their lives that require correction. I know that a soft answer turns away anger, but I confess that I don't always answer softly. Give me Your softness.

Make me a mother who listens to the concerns and questions my children bring to me. Help me to be quick to listen, slow to speak, and slow to get angry. Show me the weight my words carry so that I can speak life into my children's hearts and be a blessing to those I come into contact with. Your words are life, Lord. Let me speak Your words.

Open my eyes to false teaching, and protect my heart from lies that are cleverly disguised as tolerance. Give my children discernment equal to the deception that surrounds them. Show us how to have compassion without compromise.

I am Your servant, Lord. Help me to speak truth without trespassing into the harsh tones of ungrace. Help me reflect Your heart for the world. You loved the world so much that You sent Your only Son to die in our place. Guide me by Your Spirit in every conversation I have with those who don't know You. You were the best example, the perfect illustration of love and truth lived out for all to see.

May the words of my mouth and the meditation of my heart be pleasing to You, O Lord, my Rock and my Redeemer.

Praying the Scriptures:

Ephesians 4:15, 29; Proverbs 25:11-12; Proverbs 15:1; James 1:19; Psalm 19:14

A PRAYER *for the* MOM WHO WANTS *to* INFLUENCE FUTURE GENERATIONS

I have set the Lord always before me;
because he is at my right hand, I will not be shaken.

PSALM 16:8, ESV

*R*etirement. In Western culture, we're all about it. Work hard and save up some cash so that one day we can buy a condominium by the ocean (or by the mountains, if you're like me) and kick back for the rest of our days. We'll slow down. Start crocheting. Maybe volunteer at the library.

Parents look forward to having an empty nest, and we prepare accordingly. But God has been challenging me about my role as I become a "Titus 2" woman. (That's Bible-speak for "older woman." You're welcome.)

Several years ago I became "Mamsi" to my sweet grandson Noah. Since that time, God has been opening my eyes to His Kingdom vision for shepherding children. When Noah was born, my daughter and her husband assumed the primary responsibility for training and teaching him. It's a beautiful thing to watch. After being a full-time mother for twenty-seven years, I confess that I enjoy playing second fiddle. I also have a new appreciation for my grandmother, who stayed on the battlefield through prayer until the Lord called her home at age ninety-four.

Dr. Dobson once asked me what I thought about retirement. "Sounds good to me!" I said without hesitating. But the doctor had something to teach me: retirement isn't in the Bible, he said—at least not the way we think of retirement. After this challenging conversation, I had a new question to ask myself: *What does God want from me after my children are grown?* In Psalm 78, I found the answer I was praying for:

> He commanded our ancestors to teach their children, so the next generation would know them, even the children yet to be born, and they in turn would tell their children. Then they would put their trust in God and would not forget His deeds but would keep His commands.
>
> PSALM 78:5-7, NIV

Listen to the multigenerational vision described by the psalmist Asaph. According to this passage, we are to influence four generations! Let's put ourselves in the role of the "ancestors" in this psalm: We (generation 1) are to teach our children (generation 2) about the things of God so the grandchildren (generation 3) not yet born would know them, and they in turn will tell their children (generation 4).

Every generation has the same decision to make: *Will I serve the God of the Bible or a false god?* If you have influence in the life of a child, whether you're a parent, a grandparent, or a great-grandparent, God says you have a role to play. We are to continue fighting for the hearts and minds of our children—for four generations. In other words, until the Lord calls us home, we have a battle to fight.

How long does it take to lose a culture? According to the Bible, it takes just one generation (see Judges 2:10-12). That's why we need to stay engaged with the children God has placed in our lives. As our children grow to adulthood, we can stay engaged through offering godly counsel, a warm meal, a shoulder to cry on, and a place of peace in this broken, fallen world. Of course, we can't do this without the help of the Holy Spirit. But God promises to give us the grace we need to represent Him well until our time here is done.

Wherever you are on your parenting journey, God is saying, "Use your influence to point the next generation to Me."

GIVE ME A MULTIGENERATIONAL vision for my life, Lord.

You say that grandchildren are a crown for the aged and that parents are the pride of their children. I want this to be true for my family. Help me to not grow weary as I shepherd my children and grandchildren. Give me strength as I teach, train, correct, and love them.

I don't often reflect on what my life will look like in the generations to come, so would you give me a glimpse of Your heart for the children who are coming—the ones I haven't met yet? Father, please help me to be a godly example so my family will see You at work in me, even as I grow older.

Lord, I pray for the spouses and future spouses of my children. Draw them to Yourself. It's hard to imagine what four generations look like, Father, but help me to tell of Your goodness to future generations! Let my children tell it to their children and their children to the next generation.

I want Your will for my family, Lord. As I get older, I trust that You will provide for all my needs—and theirs. I cast all my anxiety about my future at Your feet. I know that You will sustain me as I walk with You since You never let the righteous fall.

Father, I pray that my family will flourish like a palm tree, that they will grow strong like a cedar. I pray that they will flourish in Your courts and that they will still bear fruit in old age, staying fresh and green.

I love You, Lord. I'm trusting an uncertain future to You, for You are my certain hope—and the hope of every generation.

Praying the Scriptures:

Proverbs 17:6; Romans 12:6-8, 1 Peter 4:10-11; Psalm 78:1-8; Joel 1:3; Psalm 55:22; Psalm 92:12-14

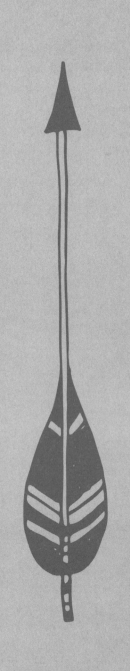

Topical Index

About the Author

Heidi St. John is a popular conference speaker, author, and blogger at *The Busy Mom*. Heidi speaks all over the country sharing encouraging, relevant, biblical truth with women. Heidi and her husband, Jay, are the founders and executive directors of Firmly Planted Family, an organization focused on family discipleship. The St. Johns live in Washington State, where they enjoy life with their seven children. When Heidi isn't homeschooling, babysitting her grandchildren, writing, traveling, or speaking, she can be found with her husband enjoying a cup of coffee and the view from their home in the Pacific Northwest.

If you're feeling tired or inadequate today, get ready to find new strength.

JOIN HEIDI ST. JOHN AS SHE ENCOURAGES WOMEN TO
BECOME MOMSTRONG TOGETHER!

BECOMING MOMSTRONG

Heidi St. John brings women back to God's Word as the ultimate source for purpose and strength. Through her personal experiences and biblical truth, she shows her readers that they have the power of God at their disposal and that He has equipped them "for such a time as this" (Esther 4:14).

BECOMING MOMSTRONG BIBLE STUDY

God has provided a blueprint for becoming MomStrong, and that blueprint is found in the Bible. He has entrusted mothers to bring up the next generation, and He says His strength is made perfect in weakness. This six-week study will help mothers find their purpose and their strength in Christ.

BECOMING MOMSTRONG JOURNAL

Mothers can strengthen their hearts and souls by spending time with God, reflecting on what He has done, and growing a deeper faith they can pass on to their children. This beautifully designed companion journal to Heidi St. John's book *Becoming MomStrong* will be a helpful guide on the journey.

TO HEAR WORDS OF ENCOURAGEMENT, TRUTH, AND MORE FROM HEIDI, VISIT HER ONLINE AT WWW.HEIDISTJOHN.COM.

CP1264